Literature Through the Eyes of Faith

FIRST THINGS

LITERATURE THROUGH THE EYES OF FAITH

First Things
attn. Managing Editor
35 E 21st Street, Sixth Floor
New York, NY 10010.

Cover and Book Design: Elliot Milco

Contents

1 | Introduction

R. R. Reno

W H. Auden and Victor Hugo were not prophets. The great works of literature are not sacred. The great poet Shelley was wrong to imagine that poets were the unacknowledged legislators of the world. Acknowledged or not, God is.

And yet we ignore literature at our peril. Our poets, novelists, and playwrights produce telescopes and microscopes of the imagination. They help us see our condition more accurately, more profoundly. Sometimes we see a deeper, more painful darkness, and at other times a brighter, more joyful light. The moon has mountain ranges and plains invisible to the naked eye. Our humanity has features we can only fully see with a trained imagination.

So, yes, God legislates. Yet we must live, hopefully in ways that are humane and moral, and if grace abounds then perhaps also supernatural. As we fare forward—and the driving force of time will push us forward whether we like it or not—literature can light our paths. Reading literature will not automatically bring wisdom. But it promises to reinforce and expand what wisdom we have by illuminating our imaginations.

It is in this spirit that FIRST THINGS published these essays over the years. Our literary imaginations need to be disciplined and enriched by criticism. Even the best readers seek guides and companions along the way. The critics in this volume have been selected because they are trustworthy friends who are both loyal to the integrity of the writers' art and faithful to divine truths.

We should not make Jane Austen into a moral theologian who advances theses through stories. But we can read her in fresh ways if we keep the moral wisdom of the Christian tradition in view. The same holds for authors who reflect the modern drift away from faith. Victor Hugo's lachrymose moralism is at once profoundly Christian and deeply heretical. George Eliot affirms a moral law that needs no Lawgiver. Beatnik writer Jack Kerouac describes debauched hedonism. In these and many other ways we often seek the good, but in partial, false ways. To know which way not to turn often helps us take the first step in the right direction.

Affirmation, denial, and judicious judgment. Historical background, critical reflection, and unabashed praise. These essays take up different stances, use different strategies, and arrive at different conclusions. There is no single way to read literature. There is no single way to write about it. And yet the critics represented in this volume share a common desire. They want to read and write toward the source and endpoint of all things: the God in whom we live and move and have our being. Read, enjoy, and join them.

R. R. Reno
Editor, FIRST THINGS

2 | Auden and the Limits of Poetry

ALAN JACOBS, August/September 2001

B Y the mid–1930s W. H. Auden was the most famous and most widely imitated young poet in England. His verse was brilliant, ironic, often funny, wide-ranging in its reference—equally at home in the worlds of Anglo-Saxon heroic poetry and the technology of mining—and sometimes impenetrably obscure. His poetic voice was from the beginning so distinctive that in 1933, when Auden was just twenty-six years old, Graham Greene could employ the word "Audenesque" in a movie review, confident that readers would know what he meant. The phrase "the Auden age" was in use before the poet turned thirty. But this widely recognized leader of the British intellectual avant-garde was an unhappy and confused young man.

Auden had been unable to believe in God since his adolescence. His loss of faith and his discovery of poetry had come, interestingly enough, at almost the same time. But in the late thirties, as Auden's uncertainty about his role as a poet grew (along with political and social tensions in Europe) some odd things began to happen to him. When in Spain during that country's Civil War, for instance, he was shocked and disturbed to see that supporters of the Republican cause had closed or burned many of Barcelona's churches—but he could not account for his own reaction. Soon afterward, he met the English writer and editor Charles Williams, and felt himself to be "in the presence of personal sanctity"—though what sanctity meant in a world without God he could not say.

In December 1939 Auden had his most decisive experience of this kind. He went to a theater in what was then a German-speaking section of Manhattan to see a newsreel about the German invasion of Poland, which had occurred three months before. But it was not the film so much as the audience that Auden later remembered. Whenever the Poles appeared on the screen—as prisoners, of course, in the hands of the Wehrmacht—members of the audience would shout in German, "Kill them! Kill them!" Auden was stunned. "There was no hypocrisy," he recalled many years later: These people were unashamed of their feelings and attempted to put no "civilized" face upon them. "I wondered, then, why I reacted as I did against this denial of every humanistic value." On what grounds did he have a right to demand, or even a reason to expect, a more "humanistic" response? His inability to answer this question, he explained much later, "brought me back to the Church." By the fall of 1940 he was going to church again, for the first time since childhood, and would affirm the Christian faith for the rest of his days.

However, the many readers who have rejoiced in the work of Auden's fellow British Christians, the Inklings—Lewis, Tolkien, Charles Williams, and (peripheral to their circle) Dorothy Sayers—have paid little attention to this remarkable man or the extraordinary work that emerged from his embrace of the Christian faith. This is, as we shall see, an understandable but deeply lamentable state of affairs.

Edward Mendelson's marvelous recent book about Auden (*Later Auden*, Farrar, Straus & Giroux, 570 pp., $30) ends with the words, "and his work was done." This conclusion provides the key to understanding Mendelson's project not only in this book but also in its predecessor, 1981's *Early Auden*. In these two rich and resourceful volumes, Mendelson has written the definitive account of one of the greatest poetic careers of the last century. The story he tells is not the story of Auden's life in the usual sense of the word, though all elements of that life naturally enter into the story; rather, he narrates for us the complex and fascinating history of a body of work, the fruit of a calling. Mendelson gives us the biography of Auden's vocation.

Not long after he began writing poetry at age fifteen, Auden came to understand that words were the medium in which he should work. But who or what imposed this "should" upon him? And how should he use the words he was called upon to use? In *Early Auden*—which began with Auden's first adult poems, written in 1927 when he was twenty years old, and ended with his leaving England in January 1939—Mendelson traced Auden's oscillations among several divergent and probably irreconcilable descriptions of the poet: conjurer, teacher, servant, prophet, redeemer. *Later Auden* begins with the poet in a new land, a place famous for encouraging new beginnings. When, with his friend Christopher Isherwood, Auden boarded a ship for America, he was the most celebrated young poet in England, but he knew that his career was at an impasse. All of the models for the writing life which he had tried out in the previous decade had come to seem empty, sterile, and in some cases repulsive. But he had no idea what could replace them. The germ of a new understanding, Mendelson shows, can be found in a word that Auden began using just before he left England: He said that the poet had a gift.

The presence of a gift implies the activity of a giver. But who, or what, gives the gift of poetry? Auden's conversion, less than two years later, indicated that he had found an answer to that question. But Auden's conversion did not resolve his puzzlement about his life as a poet: What should he do with the gift that God had given him? During the war years, from his apartment in New York, his pursuit of an answer to that question led him upon a remarkable intellectual and spiritual journey. In reviews and essays commissioned by major American periodicals, he would explore thinkers and ideas that he hoped would help him figure out what he was supposed to do, as a poet and a man: He considered Kierkegaard, Reinhold Niebuhr, and Paul Tillich, along with a host of less well-known figures like the historian Charles Norris Cochrane and, a little later on, the polymathic but eccentric philosopher–historian Eugen Rosenstock-Huessy.

As Mendelson demonstrates, Auden's essays and reviews consistently depicted these figures as having some significant contribution to make to the interpretation of Western culture at that particular and terrible moment. But in the poems Auden was writing at the same time, Mendelson convincingly argues, he was preoccupied with the questions he could not answer, with the doubts that even the greatest of his intellectual helpers left unassuaged. Among these poems are some of Auden's finest achievements, including the three long poems he wrote between 1941 and 1947, "For the Time Being: A Christmas Oratorio," "The Sea and the Mirror: A Commentary on *The Tempest*," and "The Age of Anxiety: a Baroque Eclogue." The first and last of these, Mendelson contends, have brilliant passages but are flawed in either their concept or execution; and even the masterful "The Sea and the Mirror" fails to offer a clear and satisfying account of the problem it sets out to address, namely, whether art can have spiritual significance. (Auden told his friend Ursula Niebuhr—the wife of Reinhold—that the poem was "really about the Christian conception of art.")

Mendelson fully recognizes the greatness of this poem, and the extraordinarily intelligent ambitions of the other two. His point is not that the poems are less than they could have been, but rather that none of them satisfied its author. In the thirties, Auden had nurtured hopes that the poet might be a prophet to—or even a redeemer of—a sick and chaotic society. In the aftermath of his conversion, his thinking dominated by what he later called a "neo-Calvinist (i.e., Barthian) exaggeration of God's transcendence," he found poetry valuable only when it acknowledged its hopeless, incompetent distance from anything true or good that it tried to represent.

One sees this notion vividly illustrated in one of the concluding speeches of "The Sea and the Mirror," a poem that adapts and transforms various elements of Shakespeare's *The Tempest*. In this passage, Auden's Caliban explains what he thinks to be the only kind of situation in which the artist receives any genuine illumination. He asks us to imagine "the greatest grandest opera rendered by a very provincial touring company indeed." Paradoxically, it is the very poverty and ineptitude of the production that makes it valuable to its actors, for even though "there was not a single aspect of our whole performance, not even the huge stuffed bird of happiness, for which a kind word could, however patronizingly, be said," nevertheless it is "at this very moment [that] we do at last see ourselves as we are." And, more important, "for the first time in our lives we hear . . . the real Word which is our only raison d'être." At the moment when all pretense to aesthetic achievement helplessly falls away, and the actors are confronted with the authentic selves which

they had used their performances to escape, they come to see
God precisely in their distance from Him:

> . . . we are blessed with that Wholly Other Life from
> which we are separated by an essential emphatic gulf
> of which our contrived fissures of mirror and prosce-
> nium arch—we understand them at last—are feebly
> figurative signs. . . . It is just here, among the ruins
> and the bones, that we may rejoice in the perfected
> Work that is not ours.

Similarly, Auden's Prospero, musing on the kind of life he will
live after giving up his magical powers, says "I never dreamed
the way of truth / Was a way of silence." But if Prospero is right,
what can the poet do except stop writing? One suspects that
at this point in his career Auden was contemplating just that—
that is, making his adaptation of *The Tempest* his farewell to
poetry, just as *The Tempest* itself has always been read as Shakespeare's (and not just Prospero's) farewell to the dramatic arts.
And yet, Auden continued to believe that poetry was the vocation to which he had been called, not just by his temperament
or aptitudes, but by God himself, "the author and giver of all
good things" (as he wrote in a 1940 poem). But how, given the
incapacity of language to grasp the most important things in
and beyond this world, could he fulfill that calling?

In thinking through this problem, Auden gained insight
from Kierkegaard; he found especially useful the Danish
thinker's notion of "indirect communication." (This is a
theme that Mendelson makes too little of, but since almost
every other critic of Auden has made too much of it, the fault
is easily pardonable.) Many of Kierkegaard's works—in fact,
all of his most famous ones—are not explicitly Christian. Such
books are easily identifiable because Kierkegaard did not sign
his name to them: They appeared under various pseudonyms.

These works approach the questions with which Christianity is most concerned, but they do not offer Christian answers to those questions; indeed, their failure to produce compelling responses is just what leads the reader toward the Christian faith that alone can provide what we need. "An illusion can never be destroyed directly," Kierkegaard wrote, "and only by indirect means can it be radically removed."

Auden adopted this approach, and adapted it to his poetic needs. In the great poems of his maturity, Christianity appears as the missing piece of the puzzle, the answer to a question no one thought to ask. In "The Shield of Achilles," for instance—one of the greatest poems of the twentieth century—the blacksmith god Hephaestus, watched by Achilles's mother Thetis, portrays our world as it appears to the carnal eye, the eye unillumined by faith. He inscribes on the shield "three pale figures" being bound to three posts; the poem indicates their condition:

> The mass and majesty of this world, all
> That carries weight and always weighs the same
> Lay in the hands of others; they were small
> And could not hope for help and no help came:
> What their foes liked to do was done, their shame
> Was all the worst could wish; they lost their pride
> And died as men before their bodies died.

A little later we see another figure:

> A ragged urchin, aimless and alone,
> Loitered about that vacancy; a bird
> Flew up to safety from his well–aimed stone:
> That girls are raped, that two boys knife a third,
> Were axioms to him, who'd never heard
> Of any world where promises were kept,
> Or one could weep because another wept.

In the Christian understanding, we indeed live in a world where such events occur. But the cold eye of Hephaestus, while it sees with terrifying clarity, is blind to some things: that one of those three bound figures may be different than the other two; that somewhere promises are kept; and that people weep with their brothers and sisters who weep. In Auden's poem the Christian interpretation of history is evoked all the more powerfully by its absence: The indirect communication of "The Shield of Achilles" has a force more overt testimonials often lack.

The Christian faith helped Auden to keep writing in another way as well, by offering him—though not immediately, and not without years of profound study and reflection—a way of comprehending a problem that had obsessed him for many years: the relationship between freedom and necessity. In almost every major poem he wrote after coming to America, says Mendelson, Auden in some way "incorporated the significant events of his life. But he confronted each time a new variation on his inner debate: whether those events were better understood as the product of involuntary necessity or of free choice." Mendelson begins his book by reflecting on this obsession of Auden's, and one of the great achievements of *Later Auden* is the skillful patience and critical tact with which he explores Auden's changing views on this vital subject.

Auden came to formulate the problem in this way: Alone among the creatures, human beings live in history as well as in nature. In the natural world all obey the laws that govern their being; only we make choices and live out the consequences of them. That's what history means. In a lovely poem called "Their Lonely Betters," Auden sits in a chair in his garden, listens, and thinks about what he hears:

> A robin with no Christian name ran through
> The Robin–Anthem which was all it knew,
> And rustling flowers for some third party waited

> To say which pairs, if any, should get mated.
>
> Not one of them was capable of lying,
> There was not one which knew that it was dying
> Or could have with a rhythm or a rhyme
> Assumed responsibility for time.
>
> Let them leave language to their lonely betters
> Who count some days and long for certain letters;
> We, too, make noises when we laugh or weep:
> Words are for those with promises to keep.

The robin cannot decide what song to sing; the flowers cannot select their mates. These creatures, living wholly in nature, neither celebrate the wisdom nor lament the folly of their choices, for they have no choices to make. We, on the other hand, must and do choose, and thereby enter into the historical world of accountability ("responsibility for time"). We know what it means to have "promises to keep"—and what it means to break them.

But we are not just historical beings. We are also participants in nature, and in that sense we too are part of the Creation. And Mendelson shows, as no other critic has yet shown, how Auden came to wrestle with—and ultimately to accept, with gratitude—the limits and circumscriptions of our natural, our bodily, lives.

I have said that Auden was deeply influenced by Kierkegaard, but he gradually came to understand that there were some valuable and necessary things that Kierkegaard didn't understand. Late in his life, Auden would write of Kierkegaard that, "like all heretics, conscious or unconscious, he is a monodist, who can hear with particular acuteness one theme in the New Testament—in his case, the theme of suffering and self-sacrifice—but is deaf to its rich polyphony. . . . The Passion of Christ was to Kierkegaard's taste, the Nativity and Epiphany were not." Auden contends that, while Kierkegaard's consciously held beliefs were scrupulously orthodox, he was "in his sensibility" a Manichee, who felt strongly the evil and degradation of matter, of our bodies. Indeed, Auden wrote in another essay, with pardonable exaggeration, "A planetary visitor might read through the whole of his voluminous works without discovering that human beings are not ghosts but have bodies of flesh and blood." And to have bodies of flesh and blood is to live in the world of nature's necessity as well as in the world of history, of existential choice.

Auden thus increasingly came to believe that we are emphatically compound beings, subject always to natural laws and yet called upon to "assume responsibility for time" by making decisions—decisions whose inevitable consequences are yet another form of necessity. For Auden, this peculiar situation is, above all, comic. There is something intrinsically funny about our mixed identity, as we try to exercise Divine powers of decision and yet always find our bodies getting in the way. "A sense of humor develops in a society to the degree that its members are simultaneously conscious of being each a unique person and of being all in common subjection to unalterable laws." And this sense of humor about one's condition is for Auden absolutely necessary to spiritual health. He may have dreamed in his youth of redeeming the world through his poetic power or being destroyed in the effort, but as an older man he found himself, as he often remarked, just a "martyr to corns," which afflicted his feet and made him comfortable only in carpet slippers.

By the 1950s most of the people who had admired the young Auden had rejected his mature poetry as trivial. But the heart of Mendelson's book, in many respects, is his demonstration that in this later poetry Auden is working "at the height of his powers," though in a poetic idiom that was incomprehensible to those who loved the gnomic and hieratic pronouncements of Auden's earlier verse. In 1948, Mendelson notes, Auden

> …began to write poems about the inarticulate human body… the body that never asks to be regimented or idealized, feels no abstract hatred or intellectual envy, believes no theories, and is moved by impulses that, fortunately for us, are not exactly the same as our own. He dedicated to the body some of his most profound poems, works whose depth and breadth have been underestimated because their treatment of their subject matter was novel and unexpected in an age whose writers hesitated to see the body as "simply, publicly, there." And because he learned to value the body as sacred in itself, Auden learned to believe in it as the means and promise of salvation.

"Means" is perhaps not quite right. It is not through the body that we are saved, but we are saved as embodied creatures, and saved for a future of embodiment. Auden came to believe the doctrine of the resurrection of the body a vital one and a necessary corrective to the implicit Gnosticism and Manicheanism of his existentialist influences. But Mendelson's argument is compelling, and if there is any justice in the world it will put an end to the ill-informed dismissals of Auden's later verse.

Auden's poems about the body are often poems of gratitude and thanksgiving. In a poem dedicated to his senses, "Precious Five," he concludes by invoking

> That singular command I do not understand,
> Bless what there is for being,
> Which has to be obeyed, for
> What else am I made for,
> Agreeing or disagreeing?

In one sense this recurrent emphasis on blessing and thankfulness is a correction of the theology that dominated Auden's early years as a Christian. I have already noted how important for Auden was Kierkegaard's statement that "before God we are always in the wrong." In that movie theater in Manhattan, Auden confronted his own infinite capacity for sinfulness as well as that of the Germans. One of Auden's friends relates that he taught Sunday School in 1942, and once asked the class, "Do you know what the Devil looks like?" He then answered his own question: "The Devil looks like me." Not too long afterward, he wrote of his conviction that Jesus is Lord: "I believe because he fulfills none of my dreams, because he is in every respect the opposite of what he would be if I could have made him in my own image." But why not one of the other great teachers, like Buddha or Muhammad? Because, Auden wrote, chillingly, "none of the others arouse all sides of my being to cry 'Crucify Him.'" Auden never rejected this deep conviction of his depravity, but he came to realize that if he tried to build his whole theology around it he would become, like Kierkegaard, a "monodist" and an inadvertent heretic. Thus the necessary poems of praise and thanksgiving.

It is in light of this sought theological balance that we may best understand Auden's sequence of poems "Horae Canonicae," based on the "canonical hours" that govern time in monastic communities and many churches. These poems have rarely been given serious attention, but Mendelson points out that they "occupied [Auden's] attention longer than any other" work of his career—seven years, off and on—and believes that they constitute "arguably his greatest work." In these poems, some of which are deceptively casual in tone, Auden attempts to do no less than to encompass self-censure and gratitude, necessity and freedom.

The first poem, "Prime," begins with an awakening. In this first preconscious moment of opening eyes Auden is (as we all are) an "Adam still previous to any act"; but he is also (as we all are) "Afraid of our living task, the dying / Which the coming day will ask." In the next poem he speaks of "our victim," the one who will do the dying, the one who "knows that by sundown / We shall have had a good Friday." Writes Mendelson, "The day in which the events [of this sequence] occur is Good Friday, and also any day; and the place where they occur is Jerusalem with its law court and temple, and also the Italian fishing village where the poems were written, or anywhere." This juxtaposition of times and situations is made possible by the understanding of time embodied in the canonical hours. In them, as in the larger calendar of the church year, unrepeatable events (the pronouncement of judgment, the Crucifixion, the deposition from the Cross) are remembered and in a sense reenacted. But of course this remembrance is done day after day, year after year, according to the necessary rhythms of the seasons and our bodies. Thus the sequence ends, not with the evening prayer of "Compline," but with "Lauds," the song of another morning.

This second morning song not only emphasizes the repetitive nature of bodily actions, including worship, but also indicates, in Mendelson's eloquent words, the blessed movement "from fatal memory to unconditional hope."

> This is no transcendent escape from the physical world but an undignified, saving scramble back into it. In imagining it, [Auden] found himself at home not only in both his work and his body—their reconciliation is one of the private achievements of the poem—but also in the double world of nature and history, neither an imaginary past nor a visionary future, but the place

he lived now.

Only if we live in the world where God has placed us can we fulfill the vocations to which He has called us.

Why are Christians so indifferent to Auden? It is a question made compelling by Mendelson's brilliant and sympathetic analysis. It is certainly true that Auden is not nearly as accessible a writer as Lewis, Tolkien, Sayers, or Charles Williams. Neither, however, is T. S. Eliot, and yet Eliot continues to hold a totemic status for Christians interested in modern literature, while Auden is almost completely neglected. This state of affairs bears reflection.

The first problem is an obvious one: Throughout Auden's life he was a practicing homosexual. After his conversion to Christianity, such sexual activity became problematic for him. His good friend Christopher Isherwood wrote of Auden's attitude toward his homosexuality that "his religion condemned it and he agreed that it was sinful, though he fully intended to go on sinning."

This is only partly right. In a letter to Isherwood—a letter that may have been the source of Isherwood's comment—Auden wrote, "Though I believe it sinful to be queer, it has at least saved me from becoming a pillar of the Establishment." The comment is illuminating. Auden tried to resist his sexual temptations, but felt them to be stronger than he was. In one poem he ruefully echoes a famous prayer of Augustine's, writing "I am sorry I'm not sorry . . . / Make me chaste, Lord, but not yet." But his determination to "bless what there is for being" led him to seek ways to be grateful to God even for his sins and afflictions, through which he believed God to work for His own purposes. Hence his thankfulness not to have become an Establishment figure. He also believed that the homosexual was less likely to engage in the idolatry of eros that is so common among heterosexuals. In his view his sexuality was, therefore, an affliction that bore the seeds of potential blessings.

But however complex Auden's attitude toward these matters, the mere fact that he was homosexual has written him off the books of many Christians—even Christians who are quick to forgive C. S. Lewis's peculiar liaison with Mrs. Moore, or Charles Williams's penchant for spanking and being spanked by young women. The Christian world has its hierarchy of sins, and may be right in its judgments. But it is singularly unfortunate that, even if we have judged Auden's sins rightly, we should allow that judgment to stand in the way of learning from the wisdom contained in his writings.

In any case, homosexuality alone is not enough to explain the Christian neglect of Auden. More important, perhaps, is his Kierkegaardian emphasis on indirect communication. This emphasis stemmed from Auden's determination to repent of his, and his fellow poets', prideful assertions of their own importance. But Christian readers, for the most part, don't want their poets to be humble: Being somewhat Romantic in taste, they tend to prefer their poets to be seers, prophets, "unacknowledged legislators of the world" (as Shelley put it)— just as long as they are Christian seers, prophets, legislators. As they often say, they like poems that are "redemptive." But Auden understood that nothing and no one is redemptive except Jesus Christ—and thus he called Shelley's famous line "the silliest remark ever made about poets." As he wrote to Clio, the mythological Muse of History,

> Approachable as you seem,
> I dare not ask you if you bless the poets,
> For you do not look as if you ever read them,

Nor can I see a reason why you should.

He sent this poem to J. R. R. Tolkien, and in an accompany-
ing letter referred to it as "a hymn to Our Lady." Mary, as the
mother of Christ, presides over the world's moments of ultimate significance: What can poetry add to the Incarnation or
the Passion of our Lord?

Auden consistently repudiated the notion that poetry has
any privileged access to truth, any especially sanctified role to
play. Poetry was certainly his vocation, and he loved it. As
Mendelson writes, "Vocation, for Auden, is the most innocent
form of love, a voluntary loss of self in an object." He knew
he would be wrong not to love his work, not to achieve what
he called "that eye-on-the-object look" characteristic of people
who are "forgetting themselves in a function." But he would
never claim that his calling was superior to any other. In this
sense he was purely Lutheran, emphasizing the dignity of every
calling before God. It is not surprising that he wrote a poem
based on the medieval legend of *le jong leur de Dieu*, the poor
"clown of God" who can offer nothing to the Christ Child but
his juggling—and whose offering is received, not because it has
special value, but because he gave what he had to give.

As a result of this penitential humility, Auden came to insist
over and over again that one cannot in poetry speak the Truth
directly and unequivocally. In one of his most powerful poems,
"Friday's Child," he remembers, in a characteristically oblique
way, the martyr's death of Dietrich Bonhoeffer. (The title is
typical of Auden's approach: He trusts us to remember that
"Friday's child is loving and giving," and trusts us also to understand that the old Mother Goose rhyme draws on the memory
of Good Friday, when God loved and gave most fully.) The
poem concludes with an invocation, and a recommendation,

of silence in the face of an evil that cannot be comprehended and a faith that, as Kierkegaard said, can be neither explained nor justified:

> Now, did He really break the seal
> And rise again?
> We dare not say;
> But conscious unbelievers feel
> Quite sure of Judgment Day.
>
> Meanwhile, a silence on the cross
> As dead as we shall ever be,
> Speaks of some total gain or loss,
> And you and I are free
>
> To guess from the insulted face
> Just what Appearances He saves
> By suffering in a public place
> A death reserved for slaves.

The key phrase here, I believe, is "We dare not say." It is not the same as "We dare not believe"—though Auden often confessed in his later years to dark times of doubt—nor does it mean "We dare not proclaim," since undoubtedly Auden often did proclaim, in church at least, "On the third day he rose again in accordance with the Scriptures." Auden's "we" does not refer to Christians, but to poets, whose tendency (as he writes in another poem) to "utter some resonant lie" makes them unfit bearers of the gospel proclamation. As Auden said repeatedly, almost obsessively, "Orthodoxy is reticence"; orthodoxy is knowing when to shut up. This is not a teaching that many Christian readers want to hear from their poets. But Auden knew what poetry can't do, and always felt the need to put himself and other poets in their proper place. Thus the wittily self-deflating question in "Compline": "Can poets (can men in television) / Be saved?"

Late in his life, he said in a lecture that he and his "fellow-citizens of the Republic of Letters"—a phrase coined by Voltaire—had but one "political duty": "To love the Word and defend it against its enemies." And who or what are those enemies? The "principal enemies of the True Word are two: the Idle Word and the Black Magician." On the one hand, he came to see much of his early poetry as intolerably careless not only in its technique but in its disregard for whether it meant what it said. It was full of idle words. But the other enemy was more dangerous still. The Black Magician encourages poets to believe that they can be prophets and redeemers. Or, as Auden put it once in a review, he tries to make a person attempt "to do for himself or others by the writing of poetry what can only be done in some other way, by action, or study, or prayer." Auden uses poetry to remind us of what poetry can never give us. But, in the end, this assigns poetry a genuine and important role, as it points always beyond itself in a strangely mute witness to that of which it is unable definitively to speak. As Auden wrote in one of his later poems,

> We can only do what it seems to us we were made for,
> Look at this world with a happy eye but from a sober
> perspective.

3 | The Sacred Heart of Victor Hugo

ALGIS VALIUNAS, August/September 2007

The Temptation of the Impossible:
Victor Hugo and Les Misérables
by Mario Vargas Llosa
Princeton University Press, 208 pages, $24.95

THE most potent philosophers and scientists of the nineteenth century—Schopenhauer, Marx, Darwin, Nietzsche—saw their main undertaking as dethroning the Christian God and relegating the soul to a mere adjunct of the body, if not abolishing it altogether. Some of the finest artists of the time—Balzac, Flaubert, George Eliot, Turgenev—took the latest intellectual news to heart and soaked themselves in skepticism or even nihilism, as flamboyant suicides douse themselves with gasoline before striking the match.

There were, however, other and greater artists who upheld the old godly truths in the face of the most advanced thinking and for whom it is not going too far to say that writing was their most ardent form of worship: Dickens, Tolstoy, Dostoevsky, and Victor Hugo. Among these, at least in the English-speaking world, Victor Hugo might seem not quite worthy of such rich company: He is known for having written the novel on which a monster hit musical is based, but the novel itself enjoys neither high critical esteem nor popular love.

In much of the rest of the world, it is a different story. As the Peruvian novelist Mario Vargas Llosa writes in *The Temptation of the Impossible*, "After Shakespeare, Victor Hugo has generated across five continents more literary studies, philological analyses, critical editions, biographies, translations, and adaptations of his work than any other Western author." One does not wish to incite the Anglo-American academic industry to Hugolian riot, but one would be happy to see increased regard, and an expanded readership, for so great a writer—and so great a religious writer, though one with a theological turn peculiarly his own.

Victor-Marie Hugo was born in 1802, and even his conception, according to his father's account, foretold poetic grandeur, taking place "almost in mid-air," atop a mountain peak in the Vosges; a sandstone memorial, the brainchild of a puckish museum director, now marks the spot. As Graham Robb notes in his invaluable 1997 biography, *Victor Hugo*, the novelist's father, Léopold, was a soldier who had renamed himself Brutus during the Revolution and taken part in the bloody subjugation of refractory Brittany; he would rise to general in Napoleon's army and be titled Count Siguenza for his heroism in Spain.

His father was the godless republican antithesis of Victor's Catholic royalist mother, according to the son's telling; in fact, the maternal family was strongly republican and proud of its modernity. There must have been some truth, however, to the politicized chiaroscuro of his parentage: When Sophie Hugo's lover, and Victor's godfather, Victor de la Horie, was executed for conspiring against Napoleon in 1810, Sophie Hugo apparently averted deportation only by blackmailing her chief political enemy. In any case, the family was riven by marital discord more than by great politics: The father was a sexual rover, and the parents separated for the first time before Victor was two; the separation became final when he was in his teens.

Literature consumed Hugo from the start. "I want to be Chateaubriand or nothing," he wrote in his journal in 1816. With the jetting abandon of schoolboy ambition, he wrote verse in a fervent daily routine: fables, popular songs, extravagances after the Ossianic manner, mock epics, odes to the steamship and hot-air balloon. At fifteen he submitted a poem, on the happiness of the life of study, for a prize sponsored by the Académie française, and his prodigious success—the Academicians could not believe his youth—won him immediate renown. At eighteen he produced an ode to the duc de Berry, son of the future king, Charles X, who had been assassinated by a Bonapartist; this gushing tribute earned him a five-hundred-franc honorarium from King Louis XVIII and an invitation to meet with Chateaubriand—whom Hugo would later disparage as "a genius, not a man."

Being a man, endowed with a full measure of heart and soul as well as of mind, was essential to Hugo, and he devoted himself to love as fully as to literature. He was seventeen and his beautiful Parisian neighbor Adèle Foucher fifteen when he told her he loved her; he signed his first letter to his beloved, "Your husband." Theirs was the love of two exiles from heaven, he enthused in adolescent transports; he preserved his virginity for marriage, and he guarded Adèle's chastity with a watchdog's vigilance, steering her away from unseemly friendship with a painter and discouraging her from learning to draw: "Does it befit a woman to descend into the class of artists—a class which encompasses actresses and dancers?" Holding out until their marriage in 1822 evidently had its carnal upside: Hugo claimed he made love to his bride nine times on their wedding night.

Family responsibilities fired Hugo to work harder than ever before. His first book of poems, *Odes et Poésies Diverses*, in 1822, made him enough money to cover two years' rent. His 1823 novel, *Han of Iceland*, subtitled *The Demon Dwarf*, did well too, thanks largely to the literary fashion for dwarves then current. On the death of Byron in 1824, Hugo's Romantic manifesto in the form of an obituary notice declared that the literary avant-garde marched with the political avant-garde: "One cannot return to the madrigals of Dorat [an eighteenth-century courtly poetaster] after the guillotines of Robespierre." The 1827 preface to *Cromwell*—a six-hour drama that no one put on then or since—lays out the deregulation of literature that is the heart of French Romanticism: "There are no rules, no models; rather, there are no rules other than the general laws of Nature."

In 1830 Hugo put his iconoclastic theory into practice with the verse tragedy *Hernani*, which defied the strict conventions of French drama prevalent since Richelieu's founding of the Académie française in 1635. Conservative patrons were aghast at, and young Romantics delighted in, homespun imagery, a king hiding in a closet, and the unthinkable audacity of an enjambment in the play's opening couplet. Messing with time-honored strictures of versification was a shooting offense in some quarters: One evening during the play's run, the author came home to find a bullet hole in his window. The catcalls and brawling that erupted at most every performance made *Hernani* the sensation of its day, and this hectic celebrity marked Hugo as the polestar of French Romanticism. His novel *Notre-Dame de Paris* (1831), often translated as *The Hunchback of Notre Dame*, secured that position in the literary heavens.

Meanwhile, Hugo's politics were catching up with his literary nerviness. Although in 1825 he had served as official poet for Charles X's coronation and had been enrolled as a chevalier of the Légion d'honneur, in 1830 he supported the revolution that brought down Charles and replaced him with the constitutional monarch Louis-Philippe. The great literary critic Sainte-Beuve, who was Hugo's dear friend, boasted that he was responsible for Hugo's political evolution: "I deroyalized him," he claimed.

Sainte-Beuve also cuckolded Hugo while he was at it. Hugo responded to the betrayal with golden magnanimity, at least at first, writing to Sainte-Beuve in 1833: "You have always believed that I live by my mind, whereas I live only by my heart. To love, and to need *love* and *friendship* . . . that is the basis of my life." Losing his wife's love, he found another's: Juliette Drouet, an actress playing a small part in his *Lucrèce Borgia* in 1833, captivated him, and they began an affair that would span decades.

They were traveling together in 1843 when Hugo read in the newspaper that his daughter Léopoldine, her husband, and Hugo's uncle and cousin had drowned in a sailing accident at Villequier. The drownings, and particularly the loss of his daughter, shattered Hugo. Grief made him doubt God's goodness, and yet he struggled to affirm his belief, writing to a critic whose father had recently died:

> Let us bend our heads together under the hand which destroys. . . . Death brings revelations. The mighty blows that open the heart also open the mind. Light penetrates us at the same time as pain. I am a believer. I anticipate another life. How could I not? My daughter was a soul. A soul which I have seen and, as it were, touched. . . . I suffer as you do. Hope as I do.

Hugo poured his hope not only into his private prayers but also into the public life of France, in which he came to play a

significant part. In February 1848 a republican revolution over-
threw Louis-Philippe, and Hugo was elected to the national
assembly of the provisional government, which was led by the
poet Alphonse de Lamartine. In June 1848 the provisional
government brutally put down a proletarian insurrection, and
with spirited bravery Hugo served the government in the savage
street fighting, unaware that in doing his duty he might have
been firing on Baudelaire, who took the part of the insurgents.

The bloodshed produced no lasting benefit. In December
1848 Louis-Napoléon Bonaparte, the great man's nephew, was
elected president of the republic by a landslide. Under the new
administration, Hugo moved inexorably to the left, delivering
firebrand speeches on his countrymen's wretchedness: "Here
are the facts: . . . There are in Paris . . . whole families who
have no other clothes or bed-linen than putrid piles of festering
rags, picked up in the mud of the city streets; a sort of urban
compost-heap in which human creatures bury themselves alive
in order to escape the cold of winter."

When in July 1851 Louis-Napoléon sought to extend his pres-
idential mandate by parliamentary action, Hugo denounced
the jumped-up homunculus in flaming words the president
would not forget: "What! Does Augustus have to be followed
by Augustulus? Just because we had Napoléon le Grand, do we
have to have Napoléon le Petit?" Louis-Napoléon's dictatorial
coup d'état in December 1851 spurred Hugo to flee to Brussels,
one step ahead of the authorities, where he would write the
subversive broadside *Napoléon-le-Petit*, and then to Jersey in
the Channel Islands, where he wrote the politically incendiary
book of poems *Les Châtiments* (1853), or *The Punishments*. He
would remain in exile for nineteen years, most of that time on
the island of Guernsey.

It was there that Hugo undertook to correct and fulfill "the botched work of Jesus Christ" and to lead humanity toward knowledge of the One True God. Prodded by a visiting woman friend, he took up table-turning and séances. At first he contacted the spirit of Léopoldine, who told him that to join her in the realm of light he must love. Subsequent callers from the beyond included Moses, Socrates, Jesus, Muhammad, Galileo, Mozart, Androcles's lion, a host of angels, a resident of Jupiter, and Shakespeare, who presented a new comedy, in French of course, because death had taught him that this was the superior language. As Christ himself assured Hugo, the poet would "found a new religion which will swallow up Christianity just as Christianity swallowed up paganism." But the Shadow of the Tomb, one of his eerie visitants, demurred and suggested that the transcripts of the sessions be published only posthumously. Hugo, reasonable enough to fear ridicule, concurred with the Shadow.

What he did publish instead was his greatest book of poetry, *Les Contemplations* (1856), which drew on his continued mourning for Léopoldine and its attendant spiritual travails and exaltations. In "Elle avait pris ce pli dans son âge enfantin" (She had this habit when she was a child), the way Léopoldine's slightest unhappiness made her father suffer when she was alive drives home the unendurable loss of her death. In "Demain, dès l'aube, à l'heure où blanchit la campagne" (Tomorrow, at dawn, when the countryside brightens), the master of aureate diction writes with unadorned heartbreak of placing heather and holly on his daughter's grave. "Paroles sur la dune" (Words on the dune) evokes a spiritually parched figure in a desolate landscape but ends with the sight of a flowering thistle, a hardy growth that survives, and even thrives, amid the desolation.

Hugo's is truly a constitution of undying hope. "Aux Feuillantines" (At the Feuillantines) renders the wonder young children feel at discovering the Bible, whose beauty trembles in their minds as a live bird does in their hands. Worshipful tremors shake Hugo as well. This colossus learned what it is to be bent double with suffering like the least of men yet to continue like a hero upon his appointed path. In "Écrit au bas d'un crucifix" (Written at the foot of a crucifix), he finds the ultimate comfort in the simplest piety.

> You who weep, come to this God, for he weeps.
> You who suffer, come to him, for he heals.
> You who tremble, come to him, for he smiles.
> You who pass, come to him, for he endures.

Hugo came to see his role as champion of the politically outcast and spiritually downtrodden. He spoke out in support of Greek and Italian republican movements. Overcome by admiration for Garibaldi, he sported a red shirt under his dressing gown and named a room in his Guernsey house in the great patriot's honor. He wrote a letter "To the United States of America" defending the violent abolitionist John Brown, "a soldier of Christ" whose execution threatened to "dislocate" the Union. His advocacy for Brown made him a sainted figure in Haiti, the republic of former slaves, whose president he warmly corresponded with.

On his rocky outpost, Hugo lived as the premier citizen of the world. When Napoleon III—the title Louis-Napoléon had taken for himself—declared a blanket amnesty for political exiles in 1859, Hugo spurned the offer to come home: "When freedom returns, so shall I."

After seventeen years of labor, in 1862 Hugo sent *Les Misérables* out into the world. Tolstoy would call it "the greatest of all novels"; Dostoevsky would pronounce himself grateful for having been imprisoned in 1874, because his confinement allowed him "the time to refresh my old, wonderful impressions of that great book." Lesser men such as the celebrated diarists Edmond and Jules Goncourt sniped at Hugo for demanding 300,000 francs—a sum equivalent to the annual salaries of 120 civil servants—"for taking pity on the suffering masses." Yet the book served as a moral goad even to Hugo's enemies. As though to undo his crimes against Hugo and France, Napoleon III began indulging in ostentatious works of charity and con- tributed to making philanthropy *le dernier cri* for a time. The novel's success also prompted social legislation in the way of penal, industrial, and educational reform.

At last, in 1870, the French defeat at Sedan in the Franco- Prussian War and the consequent fall of Napoleon III cleared the way for Hugo's return to his native land. He received a hero's welcome. Honorific delegations of writers and statesmen came knocking at his door; women market workers from Les Halles draped him in flowers. The journal he kept during the siege of Paris records a straitened diet featuring dog or perhaps even rat—"We are eating the Unknown"—but Hugo made the most of wartime conditions in other respects, demanding a more refined and substantial daily ration when it came to sex: Pushing seventy years old, he totted up forty different sexual partners in the course of five months; the sex log he had kept faithfully throughout his life—and which lists encounters with hundreds of women—certifies the liaisons. The fiercely virginal youth and devoted young husband had devolved into a satyr, and Parisian womanhood was honored to provide its literary hero with the services he required.

The Paris honeymoon did not last long. With the bloody suppression of the socialist Commune in May 1871, Hugo found himself once again on treacherous ground in France. This time Brussels was no better: When Hugo offered asy- lum in his house there to any political refugees, a well-heeled mob raged outside his home, chanted "Death to Victor Hugo! Death to Jean Valjean!" smashed the windows, and attempted to batter the door down. The next morning, the Hugos were banished from Belgium for disturbing the peace. He returned to Paris for a brief spell, but the scene disgusted him, and Guernsey offered refuge once more. He turned again to political fleering in the poems of *L'Année Terrible*, decrying the stupid fatality of history, in which one tyrant succeeds another, as though men had no control over their own destiny. A novel of the French Revolution, *Quatrevingt-treize*, followed in short order.

In 1873, however, encouraged by political developments, he found his way back to Paris, where he would live out his life. A stroke in 1878 hurt him, though he rallied a year later with some impressive verses. On his eightieth birthday, in 1882, a half million people passed in procession before him as he sat at the window of his house.

His death in 1885 was even more of a celebrity spectacle. His spiritual condition as the end approached became a national concern. In a newspaper cartoon, the archbishop of Paris kept vigil on Hugo's roof with a butterfly net, eager to snatch the writer's departing soul; however, the anticlerical Hugo, who had never been baptized but had nonetheless enjoyed direct access to Christ, Moses, and Muhammad, was not about to fold at the last moment. "I shall close my terrestrial eye, but the spiritual eye will remain open, wider than ever. I reject the prayers of all churches. I ask for a prayer from every soul."

A hurried parliamentary order deconsecrated the Church of Saint Geneviève and rededicated it (for the fourth time in a spiritually contentious history) as the Pantheon, where the bones of venerable Frenchmen were to repose in secular glory. The remains of this secular saint and patron of the wretched of the earth rode to the place of honor in a pauper's hearse. A police source informed Edmond Goncourt that the brothels were shuttered and the city's prostitutes had bedecked their crotches with black crepe in honor of the great man's passing. More than two million people, more than the population of Paris, joined in the funeral procession. No other writer before or since has known such an outpouring.

Although Hugo wrote 158,000 lines of verse and retains to this day the reputation as France's premier poet (when asked who most deserved that distinction, André Gide replied, "Victor Hugo, alas," that archaic lavender sigh being a favored Hugolian interjection), there can be little question that his masterwork, and one of the greatest novels of the nineteenth century, is *Les Misérables.* It is a 1,200-page monument of a book with a peerless moral giant as hero and the vaulting ambition to transform the world through love.

Aesthetic exquisites will find the novel rough-hewn and perhaps uncouth, even if they acknowledge its oceanic power. Lytton Strachey called it "the most magnificent failure—the most 'wild enormity' ever produced by a man of genius." Contrary to Flaubertian example, Hugo demonstrates that a great novel is to be made, not of perfectly flowing ironic sentences, but rather of thudding emotional jolts, transparent plot contrivances, and good and evil in mortal combat. Simple feelings wrung for all they're worth are the fundamentals of Hugo's art, and any reader who does not tear up at the splendor with which Jean Valjean triumphs over his agonies has failed truly to understand the book's teaching.

As most everyone knows, Jean Valjean is a decent man sentenced to five years' imprisonment in the galleys for stealing a loaf of bread to feed his sister's seven children; several escape attempts stretch his sentence out to nineteen years. Hatred of society's injustice toward him breeds hatred of God's cruelty, and Jean Valjean leaves prison a hard and bitter soul.

The novel recounts his fearsome path toward salvation. A saintly bishop's merciful kindness leads Valjean to amend his life, and he becomes a factory owner under the name Monsieur Madeleine, whose industrial innovation brings prosperity to his town, which rewards him by making him mayor. He tangles with the police officer Javert over the fate of Fantine, a young woman who in desperation has become a prostitute. No one believes more devoutly in the rightness of the social order, including the hell at the bottom, than Javert; no one believes more devoutly in the redemptive power of love than Valjean, who takes it upon himself to act like beneficent Providence because he knows what it is to be nothing in the world's eyes.

He becomes nothing once again when another man, Champmathieu, believed to be Jean Valjean, is about to be sentenced to life imprisonment and conscience moves the real Valjean to announce himself. The law has a long memory, and an ancient petty theft lands Valjean in the galleys once again. After a daring escape several years later, Valjean keeps his pledge to the dying Fantine by fetching her little girl, Cosette, who has been monstrously abused by her keepers, the Thénardiers. Valjean's and Cosette's is the tender encounter of two souls desperate for love, and they live in Paris as father and daughter, sometimes under the name Leblanc, their happiness threatened periodically by the relentless nosings of Javert and the criminal perfidy of the Thenardiers.

Their simple contentment is complicated when Marius Pontmercy falls in love with Cosette. Marius's pining for Cosette affords Hugo the opportunity for an excursus on how the loving soul outranks the disinterested mind when it comes to comprehending the essential truth about life:

> Happy, even in anguish, is he to whom God has given
> a soul worthy of love and of grief! He who has not seen
> the things of this world, and the hearts of men by this
> double light, has seen nothing, and knows nothing of
> the truth. The soul which loves and suffers is in this
> sublime state.

Marius's finding Cosette, and finding his love reciprocated, affords Hugo the opportunity to extol human love as of the utmost magnificence; the really quite commonplace details of the pure and youthful heart in bloom swell into a lavish moral spectacle:

> Destiny, with its mysterious and fatal patience, was
> slowly bringing these two beings near each other, fully
> charged and all languishing with the stormy electric-
> ities of passion—these two souls which held love as
> two clouds hold lightning, and which were to meet
> and mingle in a glance like clouds in a flash.

When Marius despairs of gaining Cosette's hand and goes off to join his comrades on the barricades—it is 1832, and an insurrection is brewing—Valjean follows him to the battleground on the rue de la Chanvrerie. The insurrectionists take the police spy Javert prisoner; Valjean makes out to the others that he is going to kill Javert, but he spares his life. Then Valjean saves the wounded Marius in a desperate flight through the Paris sewers; Javert is waiting to snare Valjean when he emerges, but the victorious Javert lets Valjean go. Valjean's inexplicable Christlike mercy has flummoxed the implacable right hand of justice. For the first time Javert senses the godly part of himself, and these novel stirrings leave him at a loss. Javert had always seen moral confusion as the consequence of evil; now it is extraordinary goodness that disorients him. His moral compass shattered, he drowns himself in the Seine.

Marius weds Cosette, and Valjean endows the couple with the secreted fortune he had earned in his industrial career years before. Happiness seems perfected, but Valjean feels himself bound by conscience to disclose his past to Marius, who is horrified and who scorns Valjean. Marius discovers the ex-convict's moral radiance too late to save Valjean, whose heart is broken, and who is dying.

On one of the most heartrending of literary deathbeds, Valjean offers his summation of the gospel according to Victor Hugo:

> Those Thénardiers were wicked. We must forgive them. Cosette, the time has come to tell you the name of your mother. Her name was Fantine. Remember that name: Fantine. Fall on your knees whenever you pronounce it. She suffered much. And loved you much. Her measure of unhappiness was full as yours of happiness. Such are the distributions of God. He is on high, he sees us all, and he knows what he does in the midst of his great stars. So I am going away, my children. Love each other dearly always. There is scarcely anything else in the world but that: to love one another.

To love is to come to know God—that is Hugo's elemental theme. Such a teaching can be mewling and mawkish, or it can be robust and eloquent. In Hugo's hands the message has a winning power. By love Hugo encompasses high romance, familial devotion, and even the intellectual's responsibility to promote social amelioration. "Study evil lovingly, determine it, then cure it. To that we urge."

To love is above all to feel what another is feeling. The democratic virtue of compassion extolled by Rousseau and Tocqueville is a virtual sacrament for Hugo, a natural instrument of grace requiring no churchly sanction. The compassionate heart must be initiated into all the degrees of suffering:

> In fact, he who has seen the misery of man only has
> seen nothing, he must see the misery of woman; he
> who has seen the misery of woman only has seen noth-
> ing, he must see the misery of childhood! . . . Oh,
> the unfortunate! how pallid they are! how cold they
> are! It seems as though they were on a planet much
> further from the sun than we.

Even when the lowest of the low must bear some blame for their condition, it is precisely for them that the loving soul reserves its richest empathy: "There is a point, moreover, at which the unfortunate and the infamous are associated and confounded in a single word, a fatal word, *Les Misérables*; whose fault is it? And then, is it not when the fall is lowest that charity ought to be the greatest?" None is beyond saving, if only the entire society reform itself. "They seem not men, but forms fashioned of the living dark. . . . What is required to exorcise these goblins? Light. Light in floods. No bat resists the dawn. Illuminate the bottom of society."

Yet the recalcitrance of social evil is not overcome by mere goodness of heart: To make Utopian dreams come true, hardness, sacrifice, and even cruelty are sometimes called for. Revolutionaries who kill and die for a righteous cause are also doing God's work:

> Even when fallen, especially when fallen, august are
> they who, upon all points of the world, with eyes fixed
> on France, struggle for the great work with the inflexi-
> ble logic of the ideal; they give their life as a pure gift
> for progress; they accomplish the will of Providence;
> they perform a religious act.

The best of the revolutionaries hate the violence they are compelled to commit in the name of justice. Fortunately for humankind, Hugo declares, God has so arranged matters that the need for violence has subsided, and men will henceforth advance peacefully on the effulgent future. Sadly, world-historical prognostication was not Hugo's forte.

The outstanding South American novelist Mario Vargas Llosa is ideally placed to lead a reconsideration of Victor Hugo, and in his important new book, *The Temptation of the Impossible*, Vargas Llosa examines the providential vein in *Les Misérables* that runs through both individual destinies and the life of nations.

> Fortuitous meetings, extraordinary coincidences, intuitions, and supernatural predictions, an instinct that, beyond reason, drives men and women forward, toward good or evil, and, in addition, an innate predisposition that puts society on the road to progress and inclines men and women toward virtue, these are all the essential characteristics of this world.

Vargas Llosa draws a bead on what he calls the "irresistible traps" in which Fate ensnares the main characters by "multiplying coincidences to a vertiginous degree"—the Gorbeau tenement where the Jondrettes assault Leblanc, the barricade at the rue de la Chanvrerie, the Paris sewers. "These are very intense locations, stalked by destruction and death, and the meetings that take place there spell imminent catastrophe for the heroes: their murder, their ruin, or their imprisonment. These traps are magnets of fate." Whereas Victor Hugo himself seemed capable of transmuting iron adversities into sterling accomplishments, thus furnishing a living argument for untrammeled human freedom, in *Les Misérables* "fate is always lying in wait, and human beings, unlike the real Victor Hugo, can rarely escape its traps or turn its onslaught into advantage."

Yet Vargas Llosa also points out that the characters' subjection to fate sometimes exists in subtle dialectic with their freedom.

> Characters cannot define the boundaries between these two worlds in which they are free or slaves, responsible or irresponsible. Readers are similarly perplexed. Does fate intervene to get Jean Valjean to arrive on time for the trial of poor Champmathieu, or is it Jean Valjean himself who, by taking fate in his own hands, overcomes all the obstacles in his way?

Such moral nuance complicates what could otherwise have been the most lurid fictional travesty of reality.

Still, the novel's overwhelming effect is of destiny in the hands of a godly creator knowing and powerful as no human agent can ever be, and Vargas Llosa argues that the reader does not mind this patent manipulation. Personal fate in the grip of Providence seems perfectly appropriate for so outsized a hero as Jean Valjean; suffering and transcendence reminiscent of Christ's own, as Hugo takes pains to make clear, rightly belong in the loving charge of God himself. Vargas Llosa writes: "When our grandparents wept as they read *Les Misérables*, they thought that the characters moved them to tears because of their touching humanity. But what really moved them was their ideal nature, their manifest inhumanity." Today we understand more readily Hugo's effect: The aspiration to moral perfection in the face of pervasive individual evil and institutional corruption colors the world of the novel, and these golden notions of humanity at their most heroic fill us with love for characters so obviously unreal.

It is possible that Hugo's treatment in *Les Misérables* of the way Providence determines the fate of entire nations at the Battle of Waterloo also influenced Tolstoy's handling of Napoleon in *War and Peace* (1869). In Vargas Llosa's words: "The great events of history obey a complicated, ineluctable destiny. The defeat that Napoleon suffers at Waterloo is, according to the divine stenographer [Hugo's narrator], due to a series of accidents." Hugo hammers home, just as Tolstoy does, the ways in which Providence utterly subjugates prudence, the capacity of military and political intelligence. In Hugo's words, "That Waterloo should be the end of Austerlitz, Providence needed only a little rain, and an unseasonable cloud crossing the sky sufficed for the overthrow of a world."

Providential history weighs the sufferings of multitudes against a single man's force and finds Napoleon morally wanting. "Napoleon had been impeached before the Infinite, and his fall was decreed. He vexed God. Waterloo is not a battle; it is the change of front of the universe." Hugo the seer discloses the workings of God as Destiny, while the great military hero discreetly vanishes to make way for the democratic century.

There are good democrats, however, as Vargas Llosa shows, for whom *Les Misérables* is a profound affront to liberal moderation and therefore a genuinely dangerous book. The poet and statesman Alphonse de Lamartine, head of the 1848 provisional revolutionary government, contended that *Les Misérables* presents "an excessive, radical, and sometimes unjust critique of society, which might lead human beings to hate what saves them, which is social order, and to become delirious about what will cause their downfall: the antisocial dream of the *undefined ideal*." The divine origins of inequality, Lamartine argued, militate against Hugo's wholesale indictment of society for its failure to embody divine justice.

In any case, he went on, such flagrant abuses of justice as Monsieur Madeleine's being sentenced to the galleys are flagrantly unreal: "The world is not like that." As for pain and misfortune in general, given the material men have to work with, they are bound to be ineradicable, and Hugo's book is dangerous because it is oblivious to this brute fact: *Les Misérables*

> gives unintelligent men a passion for the impossible: the most terrible and the most homicidal of passions that one can instill in the masses is the passion for the impossible. Because everything is impossible in the aspirations of *Les Misérables*, and the main impossibility is that all our suffering will disappear.

Lamartine's is really the sensible voice of liberal democracy, which does not expect moral heroism of its citizens or perfect justice of its society. Vargas Llosa in both his literary and political careers—he ran unsuccessfully for president of Peru in 1990, advocating democratic values, including a turn toward a free-market economy—has possessed just such a voice himself. In the 1991 essay "Saul Bellow and Chinese Whispers," collected in *Making Waves*, he assails the "Deng Xiaopings, Fidel Castros, ayatollahs, Kim Il Sungs and their like still loose in the world. They have tried to bring the heavens to the earth and like all those who have attempted to do so, they have created unliveable societies." Yet, in his new book, Vargas Llosa plainly comes down on the side of the utopian visionary Victor Hugo against Lamartine, whom he likens to the agents of the Spanish Inquisition.

Why then this volte-face, which makes a hero of the immoderate Hugo and a villain of the moderate Lamartine? Vargas Llosa appears to think that, as Hugo's novel has served as moral armament to enemies of tyranny, so anyone who finds his socialist utopianism seriously objectionable must be taking the side of tyrants. Here it is a matter of excess responding to the excess that was in turn responding to excess: Vargas Llosa's to Lamartine's to Hugo's.

Vargas Llosa is absolutely right, however, in recognizing that there is moral beauty in Hugo's vision, to which Lamartine, in meanness of spirit, seems altogether blind: "There is no doubt . . . that in the history of literature, *Les Misérables* is one of the works that have been most influential in making so many men and women of all languages and cultures desire a more just, rational, and beautiful world than the one they live in."

To love the radiance in the heart of Jean Valjean, and perhaps even of the insurrectionists on the barricades, is not the same as to adopt a political program or call the troops to arms. Hugo was not writing a political tract but what he explicitly called "a religious book." *Les Misérables* is above all a testament to human goodness and to the mysterious goodness of a God who allows terrible suffering as men struggle to perfect their souls, and who loves men all the more for their struggle.

4 | The End of the Road

R. R. Reno, October 2008

THE road dominates the American imagination, from the Oregon Trail to Route 66. That strange, in-between time of escape, freedom, and adventure: On the road, you leave behind all the ordinary routines and demands. Still, I was surprised when my daughter was assigned *On the Road* in her high-school English class. Kerouac's frenetic novel seemed less obvious a choice than *Moby Dick* and less safe a choice than *To Kill a Mockingbird*.

But I soon discovered that my daughter's assignment reflects a new consensus about American literature. The Library of America series put out a Kerouac volume last year, on the fiftieth anniversary of the publication of *On the Road* in 1957. A number of other books devoted to Kerouac and *On the Road* hit the shelves of the big bookstore chains. Literary journals published retrospectives. These signs point to a remarkable fact: Jack Kerouac's evocation of the rag-tag beatnik culture of his day has entered the canon of Great American Novels.

On the Road is a thinly fictionalized account of Kerouac's road trips in the late 1940s. A talented working-class kid from Lowell, Massachusetts, Kerouac was recruited to play football at Columbia University in 1941. After two years he dropped out to become a writer, living in New York as the proverbial struggling artist.

It was there he met Allen Ginsberg, William S. Burroughs, and other poets, writers, and wandering souls. Kerouac dubbed his little group the Beats. The name came from a slang term for down and out, but, when applied to the literary crowd, it came to capture the ragged, free-spirited existence of those who live on the edges of society. After the traumas of the Great Depression and World War II, the vast majority of Americans eagerly returned to the relative stability of middle-class life, now reaching outward to the newly emerging suburbs. The Beats were the first wave of rebellion against this larger trend. They self-consciously set themselves against the postwar push toward normalcy by surviving on odd jobs, G.I. benefits, and donations from friends and family.

On the Road opens in this New York scene of aspiring poets, writers, and seekers. The narrator, Sal Paradise, is trying to make his way as a young writer. But life has become suffused with the "feeling that everything was dead." (In real life, Kerouac's father died in 1946.) The would-be young sages have reached various dead ends. "All my New York friends," Sal reports, "were in the negative, nightmare position of putting down society and giving their tired bookish or political or psychoanalytical reasons."

But a new possibility appears when there arrives in town a man named Dean Moriarty—based on Neal Cassady, a charismatic personality of great importance in the history of the Beats. Abandoned child of a drunk in Denver, sometime resident of reform schools, and con man, Dean is a man of unaccountable energies and appetites. The incarnation of pure American freedom, he casts his spell over Sal's circle of friends. His zest for life galvanizes the seeking literary types living in dank walk-ups in Manhattan. But Dean leaves, and, in leaving, he becomes the lure that draws Sal out of New York and onto the road.

The body of the novel is divided into four main road trips, three crossing and re-crossing the United States, and the fourth from Denver down to Mexico City. Sal narrates his adventures in the fast-paced fashion of *this happened* and then *that happened*. He meets oddball characters. There are numerous stops and side adventures. And yet, the story comes quickly to focus on Dean. No matter where the road leads, it inevitably involves finding Dean, being found by Dean, launching out on cross-country drives with Dean, partying all night with Dean, and finally, in Mexico City, being abandoned by Dean.

Kerouac is not subtle about Dean's role. Although Dean steals without hesitation, cheats on his women, ignores his children, and abandons Sal when he is sick, Dean has "the tremendous energy of a new kind of American saint." "Behind him charred ruins smoked," the narrator tells the reader, but Dean rises out of the chaos he creates with a "ragged W. C. Fields saintliness." Soaked in sweat, muddy, and reeking of urine, Dean radiates "the purity of the road." Despite Dean's erratic, destructive, and selfish behavior, Kerouac describes his achievement with clarity: "Bitterness, recriminations, advice, morality, sadness—everything was behind him, and ahead of him was the ragged and ecstatic joy of pure being." The quintessential free spirit, he has the power to turn his back on all the hindering limitations that ordinary folks feel so acutely, the most limiting of which are moral conventions. "The thing," he preaches, "is not to get hung up."

As Kerouac tells us in a moment of revelation, "I suddenly realized that Dean, by virtue of his enormous series of sins, was becoming the Idiot, the Imbecile, the Saint." The rhetoric of holiness so closely combined with sordid behavior can outrage the pious reader of *On the Road*, but it should not surprise. Kerouac is following a long literary tradition of juxtaposing high and low, sacred and profane, noble and base. Sal writes in order to convey his "reverent mad feelings." Dean is angelic in his "rages and furies," and Sal records that, in a night of revelry, "Dean became frantically and demonically and seraphically drunk." Dean is a con man and a wise man, a mystical lecher, a debauched embodiment of spiritual purity.

The problem of happiness is at once social and existential. As Jean-Jacques Rousseau observed early in the modern era, social expectations alienate. The examples are many. Good manners dictate saying "thank you" even when we are not truly grateful. Prudence and anxiety about the dire consequences of poverty encourage us to save for the future and resist the temptation to spend for the pleasures of the moment. Conventional morality condemns as sinful those actions that are based on some of the immediate sexual desires of men and women. In each case, and in countless others, what we think and feel and want are at odds with what is expected.

Rousseau was a complicated thinker. His theory of the social contract can give the impression that he endorses the classical picture of happiness as socialization into a community of virtue. But in his influential dramatizations of the good life, *Emile* and *La Nouvelle Héloïse*, he outlined a new approach. Those who wish to live well must break the charm of social conventions so that they can live according to their truest impulses and innermost desires.

The bohemians followed Rousseau's advice in nineteenth-century Paris. Henry David Thoreau and Walt Whitman were New World bohemians, and in the twentieth century the tenements of Greenwich Village became an important center of

American bohemian life. The personalities, motivations, and literary movements were different in each case, but they all viewed the rigid social and moral conventions of respectable society as impoverishing and unnecessary.

Rousseau's counsel and the bohemian approach to life can seem an easy hedonism, but it never has been, or at least never merely. Rousseau knew that man is a social animal. We are hardwired to want to live in accord with social conventions. As a result, any sort of deviance that is intentional rather than pathological has a heroic magnificence—a status Rousseau proudly assigned to himself. Not surprisingly, then, one of the signal features of the bohemian project has been a celebration of transgression for its own sake. Those who break the rules—whether artistic, literary, or moral—gain the most admiration, because they have demonstrated their self-willed freedom from society.

The Beats were quintessential bohemians who felt the plain-Jane expectations of middle-class American life as an infecting, constraining force. Wife, career, mortgage, children, savings accounts, and quiet suburban streets: These were realities overlaid by the deadening expectations of conventional morality. Escape was essential, and, although Kerouac and the other Beats lacked Rousseau's clarity about the constant impulse of human nature to accept and submit to social authority, they intuitively recognized the need for dramatic acts and symbols of transgression.

All of this makes it wrong to read *On the Road* as a story of adolescent self-indulgence and thrill-seeking. Just as St. Francis tore off his clothes in the city square and rejected life according to normal hopes and fears, so Dean is a man entirely outside society. His criminality is not motivated by a mean desire for money. He does not steal cars to sell them, for that would simply be a dishonest way of getting the equivalent of a regu-

lar paycheck. Dean commits crimes because it is in his nature
to grab whatever is at hand to enjoy the moment. His transgressions, Kerouac tells us, were all part of "a wild yea-saying
overburst of American joy." Dean wants to live, and, as Jesus
advises, he worries not about the morrow—while he pops pills,
smokes joints, and downs shots of whiskey. In his conscience-
less carelessness, Dean is angelic. "He was BEAT—the root, the
soul of Beatific," living in the moment, one tap of the cymbal
at a time.

In 1957, the *New York Times* review hailed the novel's publication as "a historic occasion." The review trumpeted that *On
the Road* offers "the clearest and most important utterance yet
made by the generation Kerouac himself named years ago as
'beat,' and whose principle avatar he is." Of course, as David
Brooks so cleverly observed in *Bobos in Paradise*, we're all week-
end beatniks now. The counterculture of transgression that
dominates *On the Road* has thoroughly colonized our middle-
class world.

Transgression and marginality have become the new normalcy. The bohemian rejection of social convention was first
theorized as a normal stage of psychological development ("adolescent rebellion"), and more recently it has been made into
both commercial fashions and academic dogma. Aging rock
musicians go on tours and play their songs of youthful lust and
rebellion to graying Baby Boomers who need Viagra. College
professors theorize transgression as an act of political freedom.
It's easy to see that Kerouac's road leads from the Beat fantasies
of primal innocence to our own day, where white boys from
the suburbs dress like drug dealers, girls like prostitutes, and
millionaires like dock workers. Crotch-grabbing rap singers
play the role of well-paid Dean Moriartys.

Perhaps that's why some critics think of *On the Road* as

simply early propaganda for our current culture. Writing in the *New Criterion*, Anthony Daniels argues that Kerouac "was a harbinger" of an age "in which every intelligent person was expected, and came himself to expect, to forge his own soul unguided by the wisdom of his ancestors." We care about Kerouac, Daniels claims, only "because he was a prophet of immaturity." "To call Kerouac's writing mediocre is to do it too much honor," Daniels adds. The book's significance "is sociological rather than literary." And then with a *hauteur* one expects from the *New Criterion*, he concludes, "The fact that his work is now being subjected to near-biblical levels of reverential scholarship is a sign of very debased literary and academic standards."

I don't dispute that Kerouac's accounts of beatnik life inspired the adolescent rebellion in the 1960s which eventually became the perpetual adolescence of our own times. But Daniels seems wrong, both about what *On the Road* says culturally and about what it achieves as a work of literature.

Kerouac was not a writer who anticipated the 1960s, which, in fact, he disliked and denounced before his premature death in 1969. He does not treat the road as a path into the supposedly real self, nor does it lead toward an imagined better society. *On the Road* disparages "the complacent Reichianalyzed ecstasy" of progressive folks in San Francisco. It expresses no confidence that heroin or marijuana or whiskey will bring us to some hidden truth about our souls. The novel is noticeably uninterested in social or economic utopias. There are no communes, no health-food cooperatives, no late-night meetings to talk about revolution.

On the contrary, Kerouac focuses on the disordered, episodic, and chaotic nature of his experiences. He seems less a prophet of any particular way of life than an observer of the inconclusive thrusts of bohemian desire for authentic life—and the counter-thrusts of reality. Sal despairs of "the senseless nightmare road." Faced with embittered friends, Sal tells us, "I forgave everybody, I gave up, I got drunk." The sentiment is resignation, not sybaritic self-indulgence. "Everything," Sal recalls, "was collapsing" as Dean's aimless antics lead to a dead end. Sal follows Dean, but the promises of the moment seem always broken soon after they are made. While traveling, Sal recalls a lonely song with a telling refrain: "Home I'll never be."

Kerouac's ambivalence is not just a matter of clashing emotions that come from the highs and lows of life on the road. The book is forever careening forward, and the story never rests in any particular observation or experience. Kerouac lists the towns that Dean drives through at high speeds—Manteca, Modesto, Merced, Madera, Pueblo, Walsenberg, Trinidad: Transition and movement agitate the novel and the reader.

Kerouac's accounts of his experiences are either catalogues of indigestible detail or surreal sketches. On one page Sal is drunk in a San Francisco restaurant. A page or two later he is on a bus where he meets a Mexican girl and falls in love. Only a few pages further he abandons her to make his way back to New York. The novel does not develop. It tumbles. The rat-tat-tat of narration, the quick snapshots of local color, and the raw emotions recalled give the story a feeling of restless seeking rather than sustained introspection, philosophical coherence, or careful social analysis.

This overall literary effect was not accidental. Kerouac took his trips with the self-conscious goal of gathering material for a novel. For a couple of years he struggled with numerous drafts, always unsatisfied with the results. In April 1951, Kerouac decided to begin again. This time he taped together several twelve-foot-long sheets of tracing paper, trimmed to fit into his typewriter as a continuous roll. In three weeks he typed the entire story from beginning to end as one long paragraph on the single scroll of paper.

The marathon performance became something of a legend, and it was romanticized by Kerouac himself as part of his later theory of "spontaneous writing." And yet, the approach was not a cheap publicity stunt. As Louis Menand has observed, the taped-together sheets of paper constrained and disciplined Kerouac. The scroll prevented the sort of deepening of theme, character, motive, and experience that comes with circling back to revise. Kerouac did revise later, but mainly to consolidate and simplify the various road trips into a more manageable form. He did not introduce layers of authorial reflection into the relentless flow of events and personalities.

As a result, *On the Road* does not emerge as a bohemian manifesto with a clear agenda or as an existentially deep reflection on the inner life of a counter-cultural hero. The Beat lingo is omnipresent, and its slogans, aspirations, and hopes are plainly in view. Dean Moriarty is certainly a high priest of transgression. But because all these elements of the narrative cascade through the pages, nothing stands out to sum up or interpret events. The details—and especially the dated existentialist slogans and Beat truisms—fall away because they fall behind. Prose racing forward, the road simply becomes a desperate, necessary, ancient quest for what Kerouac describes in a number of places as "the pearl."

That feeling—of straining, desperate, and failed seeking—does not define the world we live in today. Our tattooed adolescents enjoy small pleasures of rebellion and collect the socially approved badges of nonconformity. Our literature is dominated by the languid Iowa Writers Workshop style: carefully wrought set pieces to accompany our studied and carefully constructed self-images. *On the Road* may have given us our clichés about authenticity, but not our quiescence—not our postmodern roles as managers of difference, not the temperate transgressions on which we insist as middle-class Americans.

The self-congratulation of the 1960s is entirely absent from *On the Road*. Kerouac does not compliment himself as a rebel after the fashion of Hunter S. Thompson. He is no Hugh Hefner posing as a heroic hedonist. Many scenes are debauched, but Kerouac does not tote up his demerits, like a high-school boy bragging about how many beers he drank. The book expresses hunger and never satisfaction, not even in its own countercultural image. "I had nothing to offer anyone," Kerouac writes in a line that sums up the effect of the whole book, "but my own confusion."

There is, however, an unexpected, subtle relevance, one that testifies to Kerouac's achievement as a writer rather than his influence as a legendary member of the Beat generation. Sal consistently conveys notes of sadness that grow ever more palpable as the book draws to an end. One drunken episode brings not good times but instead memories of an earlier, urine-soaked and unconscious night on the floor of a men's room. The road of transgressive freedom seems haunted by defilement. Sal's final visions in Mexico City do not come from any high at all, but instead from fever-induced delusions as Dean leaves him. Sickness and abandonment take the place of the promised adventure and fellowship of the road.

Most poignantly of all, the novel opens with voluble talk about Nietzsche and Schopenhauer and Proust, but it concludes with Dean's strange, incoherent effusions. By the end, Sal tells us, "He couldn't talk any more. He hopped and laughed, he stuttered and fluttered his hands and said,

'Ah—aha—you must hear.' We listened, all ears. But he forgot what he wanted to say." Dean's mind is so fried by drugs and alcohol that he can no longer carry on a conversation. The seraphic mystic of "pure love" becomes a mute oracle. The great bohemian guru can no longer offer guidance. One feels the need for the road in Kerouac's forward-leaning prose. But the reader also feels the failure. "I think of Dean Moriarty," Sal the narrator writes in his final line, "I even think of Old Dean Moriarty the father we never found." Then, as if wishing to ward off the demons of emptiness and loss, Sal repeats, "I think of Dean Moriarty."

The sad sense of failure and decay in *On the Road* strikes me as far more contemporary than the revelry and debauchery of the novel. We have not inherited Dean's "wild yea-saying overburst of American joy," nor have we found our way to the "joy of pure being." True enough, we smile and congratulate ourselves for our progressive attitudes as we accommodate ourselves to a society committed to embracing any number of strange "lifestyle choices." But on the whole, our culture seems dominated by worries. The media lust for bad tidings, as if to insist that we must suffer for failing to find the pearl of great price. At leading universities, one can be forgiven for concluding that our academic leaders believe that Western culture does not deserve to thrive or even to survive—a thought held even as they ride along the surfaces of a remarkable social tolerance, born of our tacit affirmation of the transgressive beatitude of Dean Moriarty.

It is as if we very much want to believe in Dean, but, like Sal at the end of *On the Road*, we know we cannot rely on him to give us guidance. We want to believe the promises of bohemian life—to live according to our own innermost selves—but we are surrounded by the sadness of disappointed hope.

The transgressive heroism of our imagination now looks as tawdry as daytime television. Bohemianism becomes banal and disappointing as it becomes dominant. We suffer the failures of the countercultural project even as we surround ourselves with its music, its rhetorical postures, and its fashions.

I do not claim that Jack Kerouac was a great writer, but Kerouac's lasting achievement in *On the Road* is beyond doubt. The manic, forward-leaning rush of Kerouac's prose drives his writerly ego to the margins of the narrative. This allows the novel to depict the bohemian project rather than offer a statement of its goals or summary of its philosophy or airbrushed picture of its heroism. Kerouac was a witness to the Beat generation, not its poet or spokesman or philosopher king.

It is stultifying to approach literature always expecting moral instruction in the form of ready and true principles for how to live. And it is absurd to reject Kerouac simply on the grounds that he fails to teach sound morals. Literature can instruct at a deeper level. Literature can show us how and where our human particularity overfloods our moral ideals.

And when it does, readers are left to navigate on their own— to test, as it were, the sufficiency of their own moral resources to make sense of the strange, pulsing, living, and almost always perverted and confused realities of human life.

So it was for me the first time I read *On the Road* more than twenty-five years ago. A bohemian fellow traveler of sorts, I had already been on my own road, hitchhiking many times across America. The book had a paradoxically sobering effect as I read it one day on the front porch of a hostel in France, outside of Chamonix, overlooking a meadow in late spring bloom. When I finished I felt a judgment on my Emersonian fantasies of originality. My small efforts to escape from the safe streets and calm kitchens of middle-class America were, I learned, part of an old story. I was going down an often-walked road with my emblematic backpack and blue jeans and torn T-shirt. I felt like a suburban explorer who suddenly realizes that the nearby forest is not the Amazonian jungle.

More slowly and more unconsciously, I also felt the sadness: the incoherent babbling of Dean Moriarty, the sulfurous red dawns that always seemed to follow the all-night reveries, the way in which what Sal wanted seemed to slip from his hands, the mute indifference of the great American landscape that Kerouac evokes so passionately, the hard asphalt of the road itself.

Kerouac's manic rush of prose lays bare his own ambivalence and self-contradiction. He did not package the bohemian experience with a peace symbol and the earnest pose of a young revolutionary of high moral purpose. He told a story that forces us to consult our moral compass. He helps us see that Dean Moriarty, the antinomian shaman of the American imagination, achieves no beatitude and has no blessings to give.

5 | The Strange Shipwreck of Robinson Crusoe

PHILIP ZALESKI, May 1995

I

TWO or three years ago, the first cold winds of middle age came knocking at my door. My muscles ached after an hour of softball and my mind turned to mush by ten o'clock every night. But I resolved to fight back. The decision is commonplace enough; we all know graying men who seek the fountain of youth with hot-air balloons or low-slung sportscars. I chose a more moderate and productive course. I snuggled down with a cup of hot chocolate, a woolen blanket, and a plan: to reread the beloved classics of children's literature. Whether this was a coward's flight from the hard facts of aging or a heroic attempt to keep my youth intact, I still do not know. I do know that it was magic.

When I opened the first slender volume, the doors of memory flew open as well. I hurtled back a quarter of a century and became again a boy with a book on a long summer afternoon, ready to tumble, like Alice, into a wonderland of words. Time-travel, I discovered, is indeed a reality; how grand that it is reserved for older folks. I found, too, that the pleasure of rereading was more than that of stepping into the past; it was the thrill of meeting a past illuminated by the present, of bringing to these cherished children's books an adult's appreciation of irony, wit, characterization, and plot. I read with two sets of eyes at once, that of youth and that of maturity, and my vision was never so keen.

So one joy tumbled after another, until I came to the oldest classic of them all, Daniel Defoe's 1719 work of high adventure and humble religiosity, *Robinson Crusoe*. As a scholar, I knew the importance of *Robinson Crusoe*. The tale is so famous that Robinson is often taken to be a real man who suffered a real shipwreck, a mix-up of fiction and fact bestowed upon only one other literary protagonist, Sherlock Holmes. That *Robinson Crusoe* exists at all is a miracle. Few could have predicted such a masterpiece of good feeling and fortitude from a man described by Jonathan Swift as a "grave, sententious, dogmatical rogue." The miracle is compounded when one learns that Defoe, who made his living as a journalist, churned out seven other books the same year he fathered Robinson. But somehow the most famous survivor in history was born, and his popularity was instant and undying. A count taken in 1979 found 1,198 editions in English alone (the number has increased since then), plus translations into innumerable tongues. There is even an 1820 Latin version for schoolboys, *Robinson Crusoeus*.

For my return to Robinson's island, I chose the Norton Critical Edition. I picked it up eagerly, anticipating what my memory assured me was a streamlined adventure tale, far from the ambiguities and complications of the adult world. What could be simpler, after all, than shipwreck and survival? The book seemed curiously weighty in my hands, thicker than I remembered; thicker in style, too. Well, I thought, perhaps I read an abridged version as a child; they must have simplified the language. No matter. Abridgements, when done with care, generally retain the gist of the original, although they necessarily deflate the art. And after all, how could one mangle an adventure book? One episode of derring-do more or less should make no difference, I reasoned.

The first sentence of *Robinson* reassured me, despite its cumbersome length: "I was born in the Year 1632, in the City of York, of a good family, tho' not of that Country, my Father being a Foreigner of Bremen, who settled first at Hull. . . ." This at least was familiar territory. I sighed with pleasure and settled into my armchair. As the plot unfolded, however, I began to wonder. I did not remember Robinson being quite so obstreperous, or his early life such an unbounded misery on land and sea, such a jagged sequence of poverty, imprisonment, even a shipwreck that presages the more famous one. The mystery was compounded when I discovered—still in the first thirty pages—that Robinson had been a slaver. Well, I argued, the abridgers had left this out to protect tender sensibilities.

But soon I realized that something was terribly amiss. It was not only Robinson's character that was different, but the very significance of his shipwreck, the very meaning of his life. What I discovered in the unabridged *Robinson* clashed, in every important point of substance and style, with the abridged *Robinson* of my memory. Moreover, what seemed to be missing from my childhood version—what loomed before me in Defoe's original text—was hardly material one would wish to hide from children. On the contrary, the most savage cuts—those that tore the heart out of the novel—had removed just those passages that I would have thought any parent would most want his child to read.

Perhaps, you think, I fuss over nothing. What does it matter if I once read a bad abridgement? But there is far more to it than that. Before I demonstrate exactly what I stumbled upon and why it matters so much, let us refresh our memories of *Robinson*. We will then be able to judge whether my experience is unique or whether it exposes a grave truth about our culture.

Just about everyone, reader or not, can recite the highlights of Robinson's adventures: A man is shipwrecked without resources on a desert island, survives for years by his own wits, undergoes immeasurable anguish as a result of his isolation, discovers a footprint in the sand that belongs to Friday, and is finally rescued from his exile. Such is our common store of Robinsoniana, to which 99 out of 100 people will agree.

All of it is wrong.

Robinson's island is not a desert in our modern sense of the word, he does not proceed without resources, he does not live solely by his wits, he does not suffer inordinately for his solitude, and that famous footprint—the best known in the world—does not belong to Friday. Even the word "rescue," for Robinson's eventual escape from the island, is false. But more significant than any of these details is that our overall perception of *Robinson Crusoe* is wrong. The single most important fact about this boy's adventure book is that it is not a boy's adventure book at all. It is, rather, a grown-up tale of a man's discovery of himself, civilization, and God.

II

As Defoe's book begins, Robinson Crusoe of York commits what he calls his "Original Sin"—he spurns his father's advice to join the family business and instead heads out to sea. Robinson is self-willed, arrogant, and hungry for exploits. Catastrophes ensue—storms, shipwrecks, and slavery—but the lad continues in his follies. "I was," he confesses, "to be the willful Agent of all my own Miseries."

Then providence gives him a second chance, shipwrecking him on an Atlantic island, whose features roughly match those of the Juan Fernandez group in the Pacific Ocean where Robinson's real-life prototype, Alexander Selkirk, passed seven years in solitude. Robinson's island is a pristine land of surpassing beauty. To its forlorn first inhabitant, it seems nothing short of Eden: "the Country appear'd so fresh, so green, so flourishing, every thing being in a constant Verdure, or Flourish of Spring, that it looked like a planted Garden."

In this paradise Robinson builds a new home—without Eve, alas; such is his penance. He also builds a new self, in the Pauline sense: "Put off your old nature which belongs to your former manner of life and is corrupt through deceitful lusts, and be renewed in the spirit of your minds, and put on the new nature, created after the likeness of God in true righteousness and holiness." Robinson no longer follows his own will, but bows before the will of God. He learns to see in his calamities "the Work of Providence," and to discern the hand of God at every moment of his life. He opens his Bible and repents, calling out, "Lord, be my help!"

This conversion does not go unrequited; as Robinson surrenders to God, the island surrenders to him. Step by step, he recapitulates in miniature the rise of civilization. He handles a tool for the first time and builds himself a chair and table. He needs a shovel, so he makes one, although "never was a shovel … so long a-making." He hammers a wall, plants a field, keeps a herd of goats. As his conversion deepens, so does his fortune. He builds a second establishment deep inland, and admits that "I fancy'd now I had my Country-House, and my Sea-Coast

House." He declares himself "Lord of all this country . . . as compleatly as any Lord of a Manor in England."

All this can be shrugged off as a crude example of Protestant work ethic: Sweat enough and your lot will increase. But this flip analysis ignores the crucial issue and the book's great gift: Defoe's account of how a civilization is born. What transforms chaos into cosmos, survivalism into society, is obedience to God. "I acquiesced in the Dispositions of Providence, which I began now to own, and to believe, ord'd every Thing for the best," Robinson says. So profound is his transformation that he comes to thank God for his dolorous shipwreck: "I began sensibly to feel how much more happy this life was, with all its miserable Circumstances, than the wicked, cursed, abominable Life I led all the past Part of my Days." Through God's mercy, Robinson's life is spared, his soul cleansed, and civilization born.

When Friday appears, the process repeats itself. Robinson names Friday, clothes him, arms him, teaches him to make fire and bake bread, gives him the keys to the treasury of Western history, science, and religion. Those who read this as imperialist fantasy miss the point: through his newfound wisdom, Robinson is able to share with others the good harvest he has reaped. He saves Friday's father and a Spaniard from cannibals, and becomes a king: "I thought myself very rich in subjects. . . . I was absolute Lord and lawgiver; they all owed their Lives to me." Robinson's life comes full circle when he rescues a boatload of Englishmen; the grateful mariners see in their deliverer not a Job afflicted by God's cruel whims, but a divine messenger: "He must be sent directly from heaven," says one, echoing what the Maltese said about St. Paul, another victim of shipwreck, to which Robinson replies with the humility of the truly converted, "All Help is from Heaven." Defoe's story achieves its ironic end as Robinson, now an agent of God's providence, maroons a shipload of pirates and returns to Europe a wealthy man, respected for his kindness and generosity.

Robinson Crusoe is, then, nothing less than a textbook in the appropriate relationships among human being, culture, and God. It might fairly be retitled, *Civilization and Its Contents*. The lessons couldn't be more clear: Welfare and worship are inseparable; both the well-ordered state and the well-ordered individual rest squarely upon the divine. Every component of civilization—shelter, handicraft, agriculture, and animal husbandry no less than law, art, and worship—ultimately depends upon a vigorous relationship with God; "In God We Trust" would sit well on Robinson's coins.

This is not an eccentric reading of the text: *Robinson Crusoe*'s spiritual depths are evident to all who read it unabridged. Whenever I include it on a syllabus, my students are thunderstruck by the power of Robinson's conversion; I suspect it leads one or two readers to their own fruitful self-examination. In just this way—as manual of conversion and guide to the good life—was *Robinson* understood for centuries. A typical assessment comes from George Chalmers, author of a 1790 biography of Defoe: "Few books have ever so naturally mingled amusement with instruction. The attention is fixed, either by the simplicity of the narration, or by the variety of the incidents; the heart is amended by a *vindication of the ways of God to man*." In Wilkie Collin's *The Moonstone*, the kindly butler Mr. Betteridge delivers an even more enthusiastic appraisal:

> Such a book as *Robinson Crusoe* never was written, and never will be written again. I have tried that book for years—generally in combination with a pipe of tobacco—and I have found it my friend in need in all the necessities of this mortal life. When

> my spirits are bad—*Robinson Crusoe*. When I want
> advice—*Robinson Crusoe*. In past times, when my
> wife plagued me; in present times, when I have had
> a drop too much—*Robinson Crusoe*. I have worn
> out six stout *Robinson Crusoe*s with hard work in
> my service. On my lady's last birthday she gave me a
> seventh. I took a drop too much on the strength of it;
> and *Robinson Crusoe* set me right again.

It's a good thing, I thought, that Mr. Betteridge did not rely for counsel on the version I read as a child. He would have searched in vain for the favorite passages that uplifted his soul. My childhood version was a most curious case of bowdlerization, in which the scissors snipped away at something other than scatological language or gore or sizzling sex. The truth was much more startling: *All the religion had been excised*. Again and again, one particular word had been removed, along with every scene inspired by that word.

What was this three-letter obscenity too dangerous for the eyes of children? The word was "God."

But surely, I thought, this cannot be. Perhaps in my youth I had read an outlaw edition, the joke of some madcap Nietzschean who took it literally that God was dead. I rushed to my local library—a well-stocked collection in a college town—and scooped up every copy of *Robinson Crusoe* on the shelves. Almost all of them proved to be abridgements. Every single one showed the same bleak pattern, the evisceration from the text of almost every scrap or shred of religion.

Let us consider a typical example, a "Doubleday Classics" edition called simply *Robinson Crusoe*. The book bears no date, but the illustrations are copyrighted 1945; perhaps this is the same version I read as a boy. The frontispiece offers a delightful drawing of Robinson, umbrella in hand as if out for a stroll on

Brighton Beach, discovering the footprint in the sand. Anyone picking up this edition would assume it to be the genuine article, especially as there is no mention of abridgement on the title page or anywhere else. However, this is *Robinson Crusoe* after a visit from the thought police. Witness, for example, our hero's journal, kept at the beginning of his exile when he still had ink. The entries for June 27 through July 4, 1660—stretching for over three thousand words by my rough count—contain some of Robinson's most exalted religious writing, as he nearly succumbs to a terrible fever and utters "the first Prayer, if I may call it so, that I had made for many Years." As the illness abates Robinson reads the Bible:

> I threw down the Book, and with my Heart as well as my Hands lifted up to Heaven, in a kind of Extasy of Joy, I cry'd out aloud, *Jesus, thou Son of David, Jesus, thou exalted Prince and Saviour, give me Repentance!*
>
> This was the first time that I could say, in the true Sense of the words, that I pray'd in all my Life; for now I pray'd with a Sense of my condition, and with a true Scripture View of Hope founded on the encouragement of Word of God; and from this Time, I may say, I began to have Hope that God would hear me.

God did hear Robinson, but readers of this Doubleday edition certainly won't, for the passage quoted above—in many ways the core of the book—has been completely removed. Moreover, Defoe's three-thousand-word account of Robinson's soul-wrestlings has been sliced in half, and—as you might expect by now—all references to Christ have been erased.

Yet this example is far from the worst of the lot. Let us turn now to the truly mind-boggling *The Adventures of Robinson Crusoe* (1977), a version that at least admits what it is about, declaring itself as "adapted." Here any hint of divine providence is simply chopped away wholesale, as if removing a cancer. That pesky word "God," which appears hundreds of times in Defoe's original text, remains in only ten places, usually in conventional phrases ("For God's sake, Smith, throw down your arms"). Not a hint of Robinson's conversion remains.

Well, I assured myself, as inexcusable as these cuts may be, at least they haven't been inflicted upon adults. Then it dawned upon me that most adults draw their knowledge of *Robinson* from abridged versions scanned in childhood. Moreover, for a refresher course, most adults would turn not to Defoe's unabridged original, but rather to the movies. Perhaps here there was hope. I rushed down to the local video store, where I discovered that only one version is readily obtainable: *Crusoe* (1989), starring Aidan Quinn. Surely in an R-rated film, I thought, there might be a little room for God. But I had forgotten Hollywood's knack for rewriting history. Sure enough, every sign of Robinson's conversion had been removed. *Crusoe*, in fact, manages the neat feat of completely reversing Defoe's intent, transforming *Robinson* into an antireligious tract in which our hero utters but one prayer, a desperate plea to God to spare the life of his dog. The prayer goes unanswered (unspoken premise: No God exists to answer the prayer). The film also inverts Robinson's tutelage of Friday: The native learns no English but the Englishman goes native, dropping his table manners if not his aitches, and learning to worship sun and sand.

But at least in *Crusoe* our hapless Englishman does not apply for membership in Friday's cannibal tribe. This weird turn of events is reserved for the mercifully hard-to-obtain 1975 *Man Friday*, starring Peter O'Toole as Robinson, with Richard Roundtree in the title role. Here orthodox religion is not ignored as in *Crusoe*, but rather mocked without mercy.

Robinson proves to be a fool, God a prude, Christian faith a sign of mental illness. The voice of reason, warmth, and love belongs to Friday. At least in this respect *Man Friday* conforms to Defoe's intent, for in the original, Friday is indeed a kind and perceptive man. But just when writer Adrian Mitchell seems to have gotten something right, it blows up in his face; for *Man Friday* presents a Friday who has hung out too long at Woodstock. His tribe has more in common with the Hog Farm or Summerhill than with any real preindustrial society. It is a blissful communal family, free of such Western hangups as ambition or competition, and practices free love—polymorphously perverse, of course. The tribe's religion, too, has burst free of the chains of orthodoxy, offering instead, as Friday explains, the apotheosis of be-your-own-best-friend:

> Worship any way you like as long as you mean it. God won't mind. To yourself you are not yet God. I do not think you worship yourself as you should. But still you are God, whether you know it or not.

In the end, Robinson is summarily dispatched back to his lonely island, to brood in solitude over his Bible and its joyless legacy.

Hollywood's fascination with *Robinson Crusoe* continues apace: A big-budget version, starring Pierce Brosnan—the new James Bond—is now in production. Will 007 kneel in the muck, begging God for deliverance? Maybe so; Hollywood likes on occasion to throw a sop to special interest groups. But it's a sure bet that the full story of Robinson's conversion will be left on the cutting-room floor.

III

It is not difficult to see in the strange saga of *Robinson Cru-*

soe a parable of our own condition. We are all Robinsons, cut off from the mainland of religious tradition, shipwrecked on the shoals of secularism. Our culture as a whole has suffered the same fate as Defoe's book; a systematic purgation of religious content. In thus assaying our lot, it is essential that we avoid seeing conspirators behind every gunwale; our fingers can point only at ourselves. At no time, I am convinced, was there a deliberate suppression of *Robinson*'s religion in order to buttress secular claims. Culture does not evolve—or collapse—so consciously. Revisionist editors and revisionist filmmakers work in good faith, but they work within a culture that is suffocating for lack of connection with traditional faith. This suffocation has brought with it its own form of amnesia or cultural brain damage. Few artists and critics even remember that people once worshipped a God who gave ultimate meaning to civilization's great creations, from law to literature, as He did for Robinson's meaner crafts. Intended or not, the results have been devastating. As anyone who spends much time dealing with intellectual history knows, truth seems to be slipping from our grasp; we are in danger of fabricating a past—and not only in English literature—to suit our present biases.

Our contemporary allergy to the sacred, and our related inability to read history with any rigor, is thrown into sharp relief when we look at the critical interpretations of *Robinson* bandied about in recent years. "Today we no longer read the story as a . . . religious parable, but recognize it as . . . an allegory of the human condition," announces J. R. Hammond in *A Defoe Companion* (1993), taking for granted a divorce between religion and "the human condition." Still more supercilious is Martin Green's 1990 appraisal of a 1955 compilation of Methodist sermons entitled *The Gospel of Robinson Crusoe* that reads Defoe's tale for what it is, a story of spiritual travail. This book, says Green, was "simply out of date. It was a mere oddity. Any audience it may have had in 1955 must have belonged to a special group, out of step with the majority." Such, Green assures us, is the consensus of "men and women of letters."

Who, then, is Robinson, to those who thus ignore the text? A Marxist hero, for one: In 1933, the Soviet Writers circle declared Defoe, along with Jules Verne and Jonathan Swift, as one of the three great foreign novelists of the Cause. Presumably Stalinists took their cue from Marx, who declared of Robinson in *Das Kapital*: "Of his prayers and the like we take no account." Marx instead upheld Robinson as the representative of "a community of free individuals, carrying on their work with the means of production in common." Rousseau, by contrast, imagined Robinson as a prototype of the noble savage. Other critics have seen in Defoe's book a parable about imperialism or social progress or oedipal conflicts. But the truth is that reading Robinson as a lesson in economics or psychology or pedagogy is akin to reading *Moby Dick* for its tips on spermaceti harvesting.

IV

The question remains, Why does it matter? Why care about distortions of *Robinson*?

It matters first of all because truth matters. And it matters secondly because *Robinson Crusoe* matters. *Robinson* matters in its own right, as a splendid novel that deserves to remain intact; and *Robinson* matters in the history of the novel. Many critics count Defoe's masterpiece as not just the most famous novel in the world, but the first novel in the world. This judgment depends on definition, of course, and a powerful argument can be mounted to push the genre back to *Don Quixote*, if not all the way to *The Golden Ass*. Nonetheless, all agree that *Robinson Crusoe* stands as a primordial example of the form. It is also, unquestionably, the first English novel, progenitor of a glorious stream whose great current encompasses Fielding and Dickens, Grahame and Lewis. As Leslie Stephens put it, Defoe did "discover a new art"—even if others had discovered it before him.

Admittedly, the art is rough; perhaps it always is, when a new form is whelped. Defoe forever jumbles facts, for instance having his hermit swim buck naked out to the shipwreck and then stuff his pockets with salvaged goodies. The text is long-winded, repetitious, sometimes frightfully crude. Defoe handles emotion poorly; as Dickens pointed out, *Robinson* "is the only example of a universally popular book that can make no one laugh and no one cry." Its structure sags: Poe remarked that "we close the book and are quite satisfied that we could have written as well ourselves." Yet *Robinson Crusoe* shines with power and beauty: power that stems from the universality of its hero's plight, so elemental that it approaches myth; beauty that lies in the majesty of his redemption. As if conscious of his role as father of the novel, Defoe bequeathed us at the very origin of the genre a work that addresses the origin and destiny of human beings, of justice, freedom, and the state, of civilization itself; and he locates the source of these essential matters just where they must be found, in the very origin of all things.

Thirdly, our discussion matters because the novel itself matters. Although no longer the most popular narrative form (for who goes through more novels than movies in a year?), the novel remains first when it comes to intellectual clout (for who would prefer an Oscar to the Nobel Prize in Literature?). Moreover, the novel is the art of the public square par excellence. By the very nature of its production and distribution the novel cannot be privatized, as can, say, painting, which made a disastrous swerve toward subjectivity after World War I and in consequence is no longer a subject of serious public discourse. Nor can the novel's subject matter be successfully privatized, as failed avant-garde experiments by Anais Nin and others have proven. True, the recent history of the novel shines with its own sickly decadence; one need only think of the efforts of French writers such as Natalie Sarraute or Alain Robbe-Grillet to deify style by exchanging moral or psychological depth for a richly patterned surface. But few people read these novels and fewer remember them. The fact remains that good novels (I mean novels as varied as *The Brothers Karamazov, Pale Fire*, and *Silence*) invariably deal with relationships between people, or between people and God, and the moral implications of these relationships. Moreover, a novelist works alone (unlike an artist in theater or film); each novel is as individual—and as universal—as a prayer. Of all art forms, then, the novel—even when a tale of a solitary castaway—remains the essential aesthetic mediator between public and private realms.

Fourthly, our discussion matters because art matters, and the messages that art embodies. It matters because beauty matters, and the truths to which beauty points. One litmus test of any society will always be its sense of beauty. What clearer or more precise commentary on contemporary aesthetics do we need than the recent controversy about Andres Serrano's image of Christ? This now-famous photograph cannot be rejected out of hand; in fact, it makes a perfect pivot for the debate about the role of art in society, for on first impression Serrano's photo is undeniably beautiful, a haunting portrait of the crucified Christ suspended in a mysterious golden-red cloud, whose bubbles and streaks remind us of remote galaxies, ancient suns. But of course the photography has a title, and it comes like a slap in the face: *Piss Christ*. That this crucifix sits in urine is more than incidental; it forms the core of Serrano's art.

Most viewers react to this photograph with howls of outrage. And properly so, for we perceive in it an indiscriminate mixing of the sacred and the profane (a confusion to which the post-conversion Robinson never falls prey; he always offers his earthly labors in service to God). We should not be surprised that Serrano's photograph has the power to shock, for even in a secular age we instinctively recoil in the presence of sacrilege. Nor should we wonder that Serrano aims to shock, for such is the stock-in-trade of much contemporary art.

But real beauty is more than compelling sensory impressions (the immediate photograph), even when charged with intellectual electricity (the potent complex of associations surrounding crucifix and urine). Real beauty is also a matter of rightness. Real beauty always unfolds in a moral landscape; it reflects in its order, intelligence, and harmonious dispositions these same qualities in their transcendent state. Real beauty never divides, degrades, or corrupts. Rather it weds, elevates, and purifies. Such beauty always leads to God, for "God is beautiful and he loves beauty," as the Islamic *hadith* has it. "Beauty summons all things to itself," as Dionysius the Areopagite observes.

To put it succinctly, real beauty converts. Once conversion takes place—as Defoe shows so clearly in *Robinson Crusoe*—the human being expresses his love for the divine order through the beauty of his own creations, be they symphonies or straw baskets. In this enterprise, at its best, we draw near to God's mysterious workings. As the *Catechism of the Catholic Church* puts it, "to the extent that it is inspired by truth and love of being, art bears a certain likeness to God's activity in what he has created." Witness the beauty of Shaker furniture; here we see what results when craft (the high art of all castaways and of all societies that have not abolished the sacred) is informed on every level of conception and execution by traditional spiritual understanding.

Finally, distortions of *Robinson* matter because culture matters. To grasp why, we must first recognize that secularism has muddled the relationship between religion and culture. My desktop dictionary, *The American Heritage Dictionary of the English Language*, defines culture as "the totality of socially transmitted behavior patterns, arts, beliefs, institutions, and all other products of human work and thought characteristic of a community or population." But are beliefs nothing more than a "product of human work and thought"? Not so, not entirely, not for those who admit the possibility of divine revelation. Here culture confesses what God expresses; culture is the medium through which we hear the muffled voice of God. For just this reason, dogmatic truths find different expression in different cultures. For just this reason as well, religion without culture is dead. According to Christopher Dawson, "a society which has lost its religion becomes sooner or later a society which has lost its culture." The reverse also holds. Without culture, religion will not long survive; thus it was in the cultural oases of Benedictine monasteries that the Christian faith of Europe withstood the barbarian centuries.

These days, culture forms the battleground between the sacred and the profane. In *Crossing the Threshold of Hope*, John Paul II makes the canny observation that

> the struggle for the soul of the contemporary world is at its height where the spirit of this world seems strongest. In this sense the encyclical *Redemptoris Mis-*

sio speaks of *modern Areopagi.* Today these *Areopagi*
are the worlds of science, culture, and media; these are
the worlds of writers and artists, the worlds where the
intellectual elite are formed.

Political activity has its role to play; but we can pass all the
laws we want, and they will do no good if our culture remains
marooned on secular seas. For those of us who are writers,
artists, and intellectuals, culture is the ark. There can be no
other. Culture (philosophy, art, social activity) has carried us
into the modern debacle; culture must bring us out as well.

Some men and women heal their cultural wounds with radical surgery. They cut off from the larger social mass and establish their own insular subcultures, alive to the presence of
God: the Amish, the Hutterites, the Shakers come to mind.
Such an enterprise daunts the majority of human beings, for
reasons both practical and moral. Those of us committed to
the larger society, however, have good reason to hope. Transformations now underway hold, I believe, strong possibilities
for the renewal of a genuinely spiritual culture. There are signs
that people have woken up to their loss. Baby-boomers who
abandoned the churches twenty years ago have streamed back
to the pews; Gregorian chant floods the airwaves—an event
inconceivable fifteen years ago.

Popular media, too, display everywhere the cracks and fis-
sures of religion erupting after long suppression. At this very
moment, more angels cluster on the *New York Times* best-seller
list than on the head of any medieval pin. Science fiction in
particular has kept alive the eschatological imagination in a
skeptical age, albeit in camouflaged form: Stephen Spielberg's
ET is a transparent Christ figure, and his return to his spaceship
a blatant technological Ascension. In fantasy fiction, dragons
are on the rebound. Can St. George be far behind? Even New

Age spirituality, anathema to traditionalists, can be read as a welcome respite from the relentless secularism of the age.

The unhappy truth is that rejection of orthodoxy has become a nearly inevitable phase in adolescent development; the happy sequel is that many people work their way back to church or synagogue through excursions into the New Age or other "alternative" religions. After all, how long can one dally with pastel-and-pink Aquarian cherubim before longing for an encounter with Gabriel's stately beauty? How long can one read ersatz "channeled" scriptures before finding relief in the Bible or the Koran? Everyone hungers for real spiritual food; it is our job to make it available.

Where do we begin? Does *Robinson Crusoe* point the way? As a start, we might whisk all secular critics to a remote island where we could see how long they prattle on about "economic man" before dropping to their knees to pray God for deliverance. And at that point, of course, we would request an essay on the true meaning of *Robinson Crusoe*.

Fantasies aside, however, *Robinson* does offer at least the metaphorical outlines of a program to resolve the current crisis. First, we must retain whatever is worthy in our shipwrecked culture. We must turn to tradition for guidance, as Robinson turned to the remnants of Christian England strewn along his beach. At the same time, we must abandon any thought of returning wholesale to the past. Luddites, monarchists, and theocrats—all of whom ply their trade today in arenas as varied as Green politics and Islamic fundamentalism—offer only a different kind of shipwreck. We must acknowledge the enormity of our task; for when before has a secular culture rebuilt itself on sacred foundations? We need solutions as ingenious as any devised by our industrious hero. Like Robinson, we must never despair; like Robinson, we must find strength in prayer.

It helps to bear in mind that it is we who have uprooted God from our homes, schools, books, arts; we have cast ourselves adrift. God, the master mariner, never abandons his children. We do well to remember, too, that Robinson found salvation in a plight more desperate than ours. Then, perhaps, we can relish the truth in Walter de la Mare's heartfelt remark about Defoe's finest creation: "Even to *think* of his admirable hermit is to be cheerful and to take heart of grace."

6 | God & Bertie Wooster

Joseph Bottum, October 2005

S
UPPOSE that words were all you had. Suppose the great edifice of Western civilization had collapsed around you—all its truths, all its certainties, all its aspirations smashed to meaningless shards. Suppose . . . oh, I don't know, suppose that it was 1919, and the First World War had just finished cracking Europe across its knee like a stick, and you were living in what the poet T. S. Eliot in one of his occasional sour moods called the Waste Land, and words were all you had: stray lines from lost poems, refrains from otherwise forgotten songs, tags from half-erased sermons—fragments, only fragments, to shore against your ruins. What would you do?

You could work yourself into a mad lather, I suppose, muttering as you trudge along the sidewalks and pinning passing strangers against the shop windows to explain that Friedrich Nietzsche had been right all along: The Christian social order has been a flop from the beginning, and the sooner we stamp out the last of it, the better. Then again, you could order in some whiskey and drink yourself into a stupor. There are dozens of ways, in fact, to deal with the situation, each as likely to be ineffective as the last. It's a problem knowing what to do when the end of the world knocks on the door one morning like an ancient Gaul with a toothache and a battle-axe.

But in those dark days of the twentieth century, in the middle of the apparent collapse of it all, there was at least one man who had the courage, the intelligence, and the sheer persevering goofiness simply to ignore the whole mess, frittering away his days by writing books like *Leave It to Psmith*, *Young Men in Spats*, and *My Man Jeeves*.

Pelham Grenville Wodehouse—"P. G. Wodehouse," as he signed his work; "Plum," as he was called by his friends—wrote more than fifty novels, over three hundred short stories, and some twenty-odd plays: a total of ninety-seven books before his death in 1975 at age ninety-three. And the curious thing is that not a single one of them mattered. Not a single one of them converted a soul, or turned a tide, or saved a battle, or carried a flag, or seized a day. He published several million words during his lifetime, and even amid the verbal bloat of our own hyperinflated times, it's hard to imagine a more pointless waste.

They were perfect words, of course. There's no getting around that. Take a sentence like "She looked as if she had been poured into her clothes and had forgotten to say 'when.' " Or "Into the face of the young man who sat on the terrace of the hotel at Cannes there had crept a look of furtive shame, the shifty, hangdog look which announces that an Englishman is about to talk French." Or "I don't owe a penny to a single soul—not counting tradesmen, of course." Or "If not actually disgruntled, he was far from being gruntled." Or "As for Gussie Fink-Nottle, many an experienced undertaker would have been deceived by his appearance and started embalming on sight."

P. G. Wodehouse tossed off such lines as though he'd gotten a discount from a cousin who dealt them wholesale. Diction, really, is the key. Wodehouse rarely wrote anything except light romantic comedy—in essence, novelized versions of old-fashioned Broadway shows: "musical comedy without music," as he once described it. And that's a genre of literature which doesn't carry the burden of civilization very far. Its shoulders, so to speak, are a little weak for the task. But within this minor, silk-suited genre, the twentieth century saw a writer with diction that belongs in the class of Shakespeare and very few others in the history of English literature.

There's something rather disturbing about this fact. I mean, Shakespeare clearly didn't mind dabbling in romantic comedy— try *Two Gentlemen of Verona* and *Love's Labour's Lost*—if he needed something quick with which to pay the bills. But on other days he'd try to work up plays with a little more meat on their bones. And Wodehouse, ah, well, Wodehouse never sought more than a story light enough on its feet to dance to the evanescent burble of his prose:

> Though he scorned and loathed her, he was annoyed to discover that he loved her still. He would have liked to bounce a brick on Prudence Whittaker's head, and yet, at the same time, he would have liked—rather better, as a matter of fact—to crush her to him and cover her face with burning kisses. The whole situation was very complex.

Once you start quoting lines like this from Wodehouse, it's hard to stop. The prose is almost depressingly perfect—depressingly, that is, for all of us who realize we'll never match it in our own writing. "She's one of those soppy girls, riddled from head to foot with whimsy," his favorite character Bertie Wooster says of Madeline Bassett, one of the many girls he hopes never to have to marry. "She holds the view that the stars are God's daisy chain, that rabbits are gnomes in attendance on the Fairy Queen, and that every time a fairy blows its wee nose a baby is born, which, as we know, is not the case. She's a drooper."

That "as we know" is simply an untouchable moment of prose. Meanwhile, "The Duke of Dunstable had one-way pockets. He would walk ten miles in the snow to chisel an orphan out of tuppence." And "I turned to Aunt Agatha, whose demeanor was now rather like that of one who, picking daisies on the railway, has just caught the down express on the small of the back." And "He trusted neither of them as far as he could spit, and he was a poor spitter, lacking both distance and control." On, and on, and on the examples go, never a weak moment, never a lost sentence, never a word out of place—and never a one of those words mattering in the least, never a one of them aimed at any purpose but their own light comedy, never a one of them anything but wasted.

Except—well, except that maybe in the sheer insouciance of their failure to be important, they came to be very important indeed. Maybe P. G. Wodehouse matters precisely because he was willing not to matter. Maybe we should take seriously the fact that a major English literary talent of the twentieth century was content to use his perfect prose for no purpose greater than the construction of pleasant farces, gentle comedies, and the buzz of language as it passes through an Edwardian fantasy world of stern aunts, spineless noblemen, soppy girls, and young men in spats.

We enter here into deep waters, too deep a puddle for Wodehouse himself to stick in his toe. "The question of how authors come to write their books is generally one not easily answered," he once observed. "Milton, for instance, asked how he got the idea for *Paradise Lost*, would probably have replied with a vague 'Oh, I don't know, you know. These things sort of pop into your head, don't you know,' leaving the researcher very much where he was before."

Still, there was something in those ninety-seven books that the twentieth century needed. You can't say modern times lacked serious fiction, or biting satire, or experimental poetry. You can't say the world was short on big ideas, or intellectual politics, or what Friedrich Nietzsche called philosophizing with a hammer. But maybe we were a little deficient in laughter during the twentieth century. Maybe we still are, in the twenty-first.

The story "Jeeves Takes Charge" begins with Bertie Wooster engaged to Florence Craye, an intellectual young woman whose idea of preparing Bertie for marriage is to insist he read books with titles like *Types of Ethical Theory*. This isn't the simple young man's cup of tea, of course, but Bertie is besotted, for, "seen sideways," Florence is "most awfully good looking." And so, as in any such story, the vital job of Bertie's loyal valet, Jeeves, must be to ensure the inappropriate engagement is broken off. "It was her intention to start you almost immediately upon Nietzsche," the successful Jeeves explains at the story's end. "You would not like Nietzsche, sir. He is fundamentally unsound."

And, really, that's the point. Nietzsche is fundamentally unsound for a variety of reasons that will occur to the theologically minded. But here is another and possibly more telling proof of his unsoundness: Bertie Wooster, one of the great innocents in literature, wouldn't like at all to have to read him, no matter how alluring Florence Craye is in profile. The best answer to Friedrich Nietzsche we've managed yet to come up with is the prose of P. G. Wodehouse.

One could natter learnedly here about the role of joy in the thought of various Christian thinkers. After all, "laughter is the closest thing to the grace of God," as Karl Barth famously remarked. And in *Leisure: The Basis of Culture* (a book that T. S. Eliot, in one of his happier moods, praised highly), the Catholic philosopher Josef Pieper explained that leisure is "an attitude of contemplative 'celebration' which draws its vitality from affirmation," and "to celebrate means to proclaim, in a setting different from the ordinary everyday, our approval of the world as such."

As it happens, Bertie Wooster and the other young men of P. G. Wodehouse's world have little in their lives except leisure. They use it mostly in desperate pursuit, or desperate avoidance, of all the young women they meet—which is, one guesses, only incidentally what Pieper had in mind when he declared leisure the basis of culture; civilization can run only so far on light romantic comedy. But there is manifestly some kind of celebration going on in the prose of those characters' author, and the result is the grace of laughter for the reader. Something in Wodehouse's stories hints at what made David dance before the Ark for the God who gave joy to his youth. And something in his pages suggests "the living God, Who giveth us richly all things to enjoy."

It's a little hard to say quite what that something is. Wodehouse may be our best answer to Nietzsche, but he isn't entirely clear on how *Young Men in Spats* trumps *Thus Spake Zarathustra*. But suppose that laughter offers blessed escape for a while from the terrible *mattering* that possessed modern times. Suppose that Christendom—the deep unity of Western culture through the years—survives best not when it is trying to respond to the relentless thud with which secular history marches, but when it dances a little. And suppose that God's grace doesn't dwell just in the tears we shed at the tragedy of the world, but also in the play of comedy. Wodehouse titled one of his best novels *Joy in the Morning*, after a passage in Psalm 30 that Jeeves quotes to Bertie Wooster: "Weeping may endure for a night, but joy cometh in the morning." And it's true. Joy does come in the morning, and laughter from reading P. G. Wodehouse. That's a small grace, but a real one.

Never was there a man further from Wodehouse's characters than Wodehouse himself. (In the usual muddle of British orthography, his name is pronounced "wood-house," rather than "woad-house.") He made an enormous amount of money from his writing, averaging over $100,000 a year in the 1920s, for instance, when $100,000 a year was still $100,000 a year and then some. But he was, in person, a shy and unimpressive figure who dressed in worn clothes and was known among his acquaintances as one of the dullest conversationalists in captivity. All he did, in fact, was work, spending the mornings editing the previous day's writing and the afternoon penning new material. Flaubert talked grandly of being a slave to his art. Wodehouse actually lived it. "I haven't got any violent feelings about anything," he once told an interviewer. "I just love writing."

He was born in England in 1881, the son of a British colonial officer in Hong Kong, and burdened with family names he always hated. "I have my dark moods when they seem to me about as low as you can get," he later explained. "At the font I remember protesting vigorously when the clergyman uttered them, but he stuck to his point. 'Be that as it may,' he said firmly, having waited for a lull, 'I name thee Pelham Grenville.'" His mother carried the infant Pelham Grenville out to China to join his father but within a few years shipped him back to England with his older brothers to be cared for by an improbable succession of aunts. ("In this life," he would go on to write, "it is not aunts that matter, but the courage that one brings to them"—and add, "It is no use telling me that there are bad aunts and good aunts. At the core they are all alike. Sooner or later out pops the cloven hoof.")

School must have come as a relief, and he seems to have loved his education at Dulwich College. But his family lacked the money to send him on to Oxford and, instead, found him a job at age eighteen as a clerk at the Hong Kong and Shanghai Bank in London. Advancement at a colonial bank generally required posting to the colonies, and Wodehouse was determined to find success as a writer quickly enough to avoid the trip to the Far East. After a rapid spate of magazine stories and poems and columns, his first book appeared in 1902, and by 1904 he had left the bank and established himself financially as a writer.

Regular trips to America soon followed (the money for pieces in American magazines was somewhat better, and the money for plays and musicals in America was astronomically better than British rates). In 1914, Wodehouse met and married Ethel Newton, a widow in New York. Ethel and Plum had a curious and not entirely explicable marriage, but without doubt she provided him what he needed, taking over all the practical concerns, leaving the writer free to do nothing but write.

And write he did, making so much money—from his books, scripts for Hollywood and Broadway, and articles in magazines such as *Vanity Fair*—that the American tax authorities and the British Inland Revenue united in one of their first joint projects, a trans-Atlantic cooperative effort to dig as much as possible out of Wodehouse's international royalties. That may have been what finally drove him abroad in 1934, when he and Ethel settled in France.

In retrospect, this proved not to be the ideal time for such a move. Five years later, Hitler's blitzkrieg swept through the area, picking up the British Wodehouse along the way—or, as he explained,

> Young men, starting out in life, have often asked me, 'How can I become an internee?' Well, there are several methods. My own was to buy a villa in Le Touquet on the coast of France and stay there until the Germans came along. This is probably the best and simplest system. You buy the villa and the Germans do the rest.

Unfortunately, he offered that explanation on a shortwave broadcast to America sponsored by the Nazis. A clever German publicity agent, apparently realizing what a naïf they had captured, ordered Wodehouse transferred from the internment camp to a hotel in Berlin and talked him into making five comic presentations for his American fans in the days before the United States had entered the war. The reaction in London was volcanic, as the BBC and the *Daily Mirror* and even A. A. Milne spewed outrage at his apparent treason. It was the worst misstep of his career—but perhaps a predictable one, for he seemed to live only for his writing, and the England he created in his fiction was as imaginary a place as J. R. R. Tolkien's Middle Earth or what Alice found through the looking glass. "How's the weather, Jeeves?" young Bertie Wooster had asked his valet almost twenty years before in Wodehouse's acknowledgement of the beginning of the First World War:

> "Exceptionally clement, sir."
> "Anything in the papers?"
> "Some slight friction threatening in the Balkans, sir. Otherwise, nothing."

Wodehouse was strongly advised not to return to England after Germany surrendered. "I made an ass of myself and must pay the penalty," he acknowledged in 1945. So he moved to New York instead, eventually settling on an estate on Long Island, where he continued to do little but write, until the British forgave him enough to award him a knighthood in 1975, two months before he died.

A number of writers known for their religious interests have praised Wodehouse. Hilaire Belloc, for instance, called him the "best writer of our time, the best living writer of English and the head of my profession." But I have always thought they did so more in their capacity as writers than in their capacity as religious thinkers. When professional scribblers run their eyes over a page of P. G. Wodehouse, they see just how good he is: The more you know about how prose gets created, the more he seems unmatchable.

Evelyn Waugh, however, once tried to reach for something more, offering an explicitly religious reading of the stories about Bertie and Jeeves: "For Mr. Wodehouse," he claimed, "there has been no Fall of Man; no 'aboriginal calamity.' His characters have never tasted the forbidden fruit. They are still in Eden."

That sounds, at first hearing, like so much blather. The Wodehousian characters are Edenic only if all light comedies, all young romances, and all Broadway farces—if all stories with happy endings, for that matter—take place sometime before the Serpent makes his entrance in the Book of Genesis. P. G. Wodehouse hardly wrote more than one story in all his books. The plots could be fiendishly complicated, but they typically boil down to: Boy meets girl, boy loses girl, boy gains girl again. As it happens, a Bertie Wooster story often stands the pattern on its head—boy is happily free, boy mutton-headedly gets entangled with a beautiful but disastrous girl, boy manages at last to wriggle free:

> Aunt Dahlia, describing this young blister as a one-girl beauty chorus, had called her shots perfectly correctly. Her outer crust was indeed of a nature to cause those

beholding it to rock back on their heels with a startled whistle. But while equipped with eyes like twin stars, hair ruddier than the cherry, oomph, *espièglerie* and all the fixings, this B. Wickham had also the disposition and general outlook on life of a ticking bomb. In her society you always had the uneasy feeling that something was likely to go off at any moment with a pop. You never knew what she was going to do next or into what murky depths of soup she would carelessly plunge you.

"Miss Wickham, sir," Jeeves had once said to me warningly at the time when the fever was at its height, "lacks seriousness. She is volatile and frivolous. I would always hesitate to recommend a young lady with quite such a vivid shade of red hair."

His judgment was sound. I have already mentioned how with her subtle wiles this girl induced me to sneak into Sir Roderick Glossop's sleeping apartment and apply the darning needle to his hot-water bottle—and that was comparatively mild going for her. In a word, Roberta, daughter of Lady Wickham of Skeldings Hall, Herts, and the late Sir Cuthbert, was pure dynamite, and better kept at a distance by all those who aimed at leading a peaceful life. The prospect of being immured with her in the same house, with all the facilities a country house affords an enterprising girl for landing her nearest and dearest in the mulligatawny, made me singularly dubious about the shape of things to come.

But even a Bertie and Jeeves story is still a farce—a musical without the music—and it doesn't escape the angel with the flaming sword who blocks the return to Eden.

And yet, on second thought, there may actually be a sort of fall that Wodehouse's characters never suffer. It's not the "aboriginal calamity" of Adam and Eve; not even that amiable and bone-headed peer, Lord Emsworth, the centerpiece of Wodehouse's many stories set in and around Blandings Castle, entirely dodges original sin. Nonetheless, the characters do somehow manage to sidestep rather neatly most of the unpleasantness of the twentieth century. If Bertie Wooster had ever really existed, he would (as George Orwell once pointed out) have died at the Battle of the Somme in 1916 along with most of the rest of his Edwardian class. Of course, Bertie Wooster didn't really exist, and the world he inhabits bore little contact with English reality before World War I and even less contact with reality as the years went on.

Even the occasional topical reference—as in the title of the 1965 story "Bingo Bans the Bomb"—doesn't move P. G. Wodehouse's characters any closer to the real world, for they live, finally, only in a magical country of linguistic construction. They buzz and prattle, rattle and hum, for talk is their life and their meaning.

"It is pretty generally recognized in the circles in which he moves that Bertram Wooster is not a man who lightly throws in the towel and admits defeat," Wodehouse begins a typical run of Bertie's first-person narration.

> Beneath the thingummies of what-d'you-call-it, his head, wind and weather permitting, is as a rule bloody but unbowed, and if the slings and arrows of outrageous fortune want to crush his proud spirit, they have to pull their socks up and make a special effort.

You can diagram this, if you absolutely have to, as the critic Richard Usborne once noted. A metaphor from boxing slides into a deliberately mangled quotation from W. E. Henley's late-Victorian poem "Invictus"—into which mangle are inserted not just one but two meaningless verbal inflators: "wind and weather permitting," and "as a rule." That somehow leads to a slightly less garbled dribble from *Hamlet*, the high tone of which is immediately deflated with the slang of "pull their socks up."

But even pulling the writing apart this way doesn't fully reveal what Wodehouse is doing in his prose. You'll sometimes see him praised for the wide range of his literary references. Don't believe it. A volley here and there at something highbrow is taken by Jeeves for comic effect, but not often. Wodehouse's references—particularly in the first-person with which Bertie Wooster narrates his stories—are almost entirely from the Edwardian schoolboy canon: the Bible and Shakespeare, the kind of Anglican hymn heard in British public schools, Victorian parlor poetry, the Bible and Shakespeare again, a few popular songs from the 1880s, Kipling, and the Bible and Shakespeare once again:

> From down the road came the sound of voices, and a mere instant was enough to tell us that it was Mrs. Bingo and the Pyke talking things over. I had never listened in on a real, genuine female row before, and I'm bound to say it was pretty impressive. During my absence, matters appeared to have developed on rather a specious scale. They had reached the stage now where the combatants had begun to dig into the past and rake up old scores. Mrs. Bingo was saying that the Pyke would never have got into the hockey team at St. Adela's if she hadn't flattered and fawned upon the captain in a way that it made Mrs. Bingo, even after all these years, sick to think of. The Pyke replied that she had refrained from mentioning it until now, having always felt it better to let bygones be bygones, but that if Mrs. Bingo supposed her to be unaware that Mrs. Bingo had won the Scripture prize by taking a list of the Kings of Judah into the examination room,

tucked into her middy-blouse, Mrs. Bingo was vastly mistaken.

Twentieth-century schooling let much of this once-shared set of references fall away, which is why Wodehouse's stories sometimes seem to readers more learned than they actually are.

Open references to religion are relatively rare. The fathers of two characters once came to blows in the bar of their club over the apostolic claims of the Abyssinian Church, but, as the narrator remarks, the wonder wasn't that they fought but that either of them had ever heard of the Abyssinian Church. There are a few classic Bertie-and-Jeeves stories that rely on religious situations, particularly "The Great Sermon Handicap." And then there are the tales told by Mr. Mulliner (the best may be "Buck-U-Uppo") about the rise of his nephew Augustine, a delicate, pale, and milktoasty cleric, through the hierarchy of the Anglican Church as it squabbles about orphreys and chasubles.

But Wodehouse's stories are never openly religious. They exist in an Edwardian fantasy world that simply assumes the presence of the clergy and the Church. The overall aim of his books is, more than anything else, to avoid as much as possible the whole of the twentieth century—its fall, its forgetfulness, its horror, its waste land. Inside his ninety-seven volumes, Europe's ancient Christian culture hasn't collapsed into meaninglessness, leaving us only fragments to shore against our ruins.

Take a look at such perfect stories as "Jeeves and the Old School Chum," or "Uncle Fred Flits By," or "Lord Emsworth and the Girlfriend." Words were all that P. G. Wodehouse had, and in one sense he squandered them on nothing more than light comedy. In another sense, he found with all his writing something worth more than words can say: a small, happy spot kept bright in a world that seemed only to be darkening around it. Surely that's enough for one man.

7 | Jane Austen, Public Theologian

PETER J. LEITHART, January 2004

To call Jane Austen a public theologian is counter-intuitive for two reasons: she does not seem much interested in things public, and she does not seem much interested in things theological.

With regard to the second point, Austen's novels rarely deal openly with theological themes or issues, and even her private letters—the ones that survived her sister's destruction—seldom speak of religious subjects. She was a lifelong member of the Church of England and her father and two brothers were Anglican ministers. By all accounts she was a Christian, yet she displays a high Anglican reticence about religious experience, and a similarly Anglican disinterest in the niceties of theological debate.

On the first point, Austen's novels seem to be relentlessly concerned with private life, concerned with "three or four families in a country town," as she put it in one famous letter. This is all the more remarkable when we consider the events of her lifetime. Though living through a period that witnessed the birth of an independent United States, the French Revolution and the Terror, the Napoleonic wars and the rise of revolutionary romanticism, the evangelical revivals and the upheavals of the Industrial Revolution, she focuses on a few middling gentry families in rural England. Touches of the wider world sometimes impinge on Austen's peaceful outposts—Wickham, a soldier, plays a prominent role in *Pride and Prejudice*, there are passing references to the British colonies and the slave trade in *Mansfield Park*, and the British navy's preservation of England in the Napoleonic Wars is duly noted in *Persuasion*. For the most part, though, her characters go about their farming and their business, their follies and especially their romances, their dances and their games of backgammon and whist, as if nothing has changed. Soldiers and sailors, when they appear, are always on leave.

Well-read as she and her family were, it is impossible that Austen was ignorant of the transformations taking place around her. She read poetry and novels, including those from the Romantic period, and she knew the literature of her time well enough to parody it. We know too that her family was directly affected by a number of these events. Two of her brothers fought Napoleon as members of the British navy. Philadelphia Austen, Jane's aunt, had a daughter named Eliza who married a Frenchman, Jean Capot, Comte de Feuillide. The unfortunate Capot was guillotined during the Terror, and his widow Eliza later married Jane's brother Henry to become Jane's sister-in-law. Her favorite brother, Henry, was a clergyman of evangelical stripe, and several letters show that Jane herself knew something of evangelicalism (she did not like it much, though her attitudes apparently shifted during her lifetime). Jane herself toyed with the idea of writing a biography of Napoleon.

Yet, to reiterate, this wider world has almost no role in Austen's novels. I wish to maintain, however, that despite her apparent indifference to both theology and the public realm, she can be read as a public theologian.

What most interests Austen about Christianity is precisely its public and institutional dimension, its role as a national "teacher" of morals. Hence her recurring attention to the clergy. Two of her clerical characters, Mr. Collins (of *Pride and Prejudice*) and Mr. Elton (of *Emma*), are insensitive morons, and she has no toleration for the kind of hypocritical pomposity that they represent. Nor, in *Mansfield Park*, does she have much use for the vacuous religiosity of Dr. Grant, who is a pastor only in name and not in fact. This hardly means that she is anticlerical; some of the most severe satire of the clergy in church history has come from devout Christians incensed at the abuses of their leaders. Like them, Austen attacks false clergy not to destroy clergy; she attacks false clergy to defend the true.

On the other side, several of her heroes are ordained or soon to be so. Edward Ferrars in *Sense and Sensibility* is a nonentity in this regard, and one fears that Henry Tilney of *Northanger Abbey* is too detached and ironic to be much of a pastor, though he provides both intellectual and moral training for the heroine, Catherine Morland. The last of the clerical heroes, Edmund Bertram, is far and away the best model, and the issue of the public role of the Church takes on a great deal of importance in *Mansfield Park*. Still, the fact is that in half of Austen's finished novels the hero is a clergyman, and two of the other novels have important clerical characters. (The only novel in which clergy play virtually no role is *Persuasion*, though even there Charles Hayter is destined for the cloth.)

Evidence of Austen's theological contribution—and of my thesis—is strongest in *Mansfield Park*. When Austen wrote about it in a letter (to her sister Cassandra, January 29, 1813), she said she intended "to write of something else;—it shall be a complete change of subject—Ordination." Indeed, that is its unlikely focus. As a result, *Mansfield Park*, frequently despised as Austen's worst novel, is in fact her greatest and most important, though admittedly far from the most entertaining. Moreover, the novel presents one of the most searching and provocative accounts of modern individualism to be found in fiction. It is a thick description of the kinds of habits of speech and personal conduct, motivations and intentions, political and social views that emerge from uncontrolled individualism. And it traces this insidious individualism precisely to the marginalization of the Church in the life of England, the failure of clergy to be the makers of English manners, and the consequent intrusion of other forces as the makers of manners.

Austen describes this kind of individualism, its origins and effects, without ever using the words "individual" or "individualism." Individualism probably did not exist as a word (Tocqueville said in the 1830s that it was newly minted), and the word "individual" earlier meant "indivisible." Instead, Austen, like Shakespeare, explores the phenomenon of individualism using the trope of "acting." In a play, only the worst actors (like Bottom) want to change roles. The good actor has been assigned his role and does not want to become somebody else. If he did so, the play would fall apart. If Laertes suddenly became Hamlet or Oedipus changed places with Tiresias, that would, to put it mildly, disrupt the play—though, as Tom Stoppard has realized, if Rosencrantz changed places with Guildenstern nobody would notice (not even the characters). In a traditional society, the goal of life is to act well in the assigned role—to say your lines properly, to do what your role assigns to you. Everybody has a "fixed fate" set (perhaps) by his birth, and his purpose is not to find a new fate, but to adjust to it. In such a traditional society, ethics is bound up with playing the role well; the question "What shall I do?" always presupposes an answer to the question "What place do I have here? Who am I?"

Peter Berger summarizes this social and ethical vision:

> A role . . . may be defined as a typified response to a typified expectation. Society has predefined the fundamental typology. To use the language of the theater, from which the concept of role is derived, we can say that society provides the script for all the dramatis personae. The individual actors, therefore, need but slip into the roles already assigned to them before the curtain goes up. As long as they play their roles as provided for in this script, the social play can proceed as planned.

And Berger goes on to point out that every social role has a particular identity attached to it. Some of the roles are fairly trivial and easily changed; others are nearly impossible to alter. But any change in role is a change in "who you are." The ethical imperative is to grow into those roles. At first, the uniform may not fit; we may find ourselves dwarves dressed in the clothing of giants; but we are called to grow into our role.

In this sense, Austen's conception of social order is traditional and theatrical. But she saw another kind of "role-playing" and another kind of "theatricality" being born in the society around her. In *Mansfield Park* she contrasts the traditional notion of social "role" with this new individualist notion, and shows the causes and effects of this change.

The heroine of *Mansfield Park* is Fanny Price, who comes from her crowded home in Portsmouth to live at Mansfield Park, the home of her uncle, Sir Thomas Bertram. She grows up with Sir Thomas's children—Tom, Edmund, Julia, and Maria—of whom only Edmund shows kindness to his cousin. Fanny is shy and retiring, always feeling that she is out of place in the house, a feeling reinforced by the bullying from her other aunt, Mrs. Norris, who since the death of her husband has lived with the Bertrams.

The action of the story depends on two visitors from London, Henry and Mary Crawford, brother and sister to Mrs. Grant, the wife of the local vicar. The Crawfords visit Mansfield while Sir Thomas is in Antigua on rather murky business involving his plantations. Henry quickly becomes the favorite of both Julia and Maria, even though Maria is already engaged to the idiotic but very rich Mr. Rushworth, while Mary sets her sights on securing the affections of Edmund Bertram. During the first part of the book, there are two important scenes. One is the visit of the whole company of young people to Sotherton, the Rushworth estate, during which Henry Crawford pursues his developing affair with Maria. The other is the plan to put on a play in Mansfield, a plan that both Edmund and Fanny object to for various reasons. In the end, the plan is foiled by Sir Thomas's return, but these events put the theme of acting at the forefront.

The remainder of the story focuses on Henry's plan to make Fanny Price fall in love with him, and Fanny's resistance to his courtship. Eventually, Henry actually does fall in love with Fanny and proposes marriage, which Fanny rejects, out of distrust of his character. The other thread of the story is the developing romance between Mary Crawford and Edmund Bertram; Edmund is infatuated with Mary, but she is firmly opposed to the notion of being married to a clergyman, and is continually trying to seduce him away. When Fanny rejects him, Henry runs away with Maria, who by now is married to Rushworth, and this is the final blow to Edmund's inclination toward Mary. At first despondent, Edmund gradually realizes that Fanny makes a better minister's wife than Mary ever could have, and they marry.

Tony Tanner has pointed out that *Mansfield Park* was written near the end of the Napoleonic Wars, during a time of tumultuous change and serious threats to Britain. The threats that Austen identifies in the novel, however, were not the obvious threats to England's stability and peace—French invasions, Jacobins spying, and the like. Rather, she sees a threat embodied in a particular way of life, one that detaches moral principle from good breeding and mannerliness. That distinction is made explicit in the book during a conversation among Mary, Fanny, and Edmund in Part I. Edmund has insisted that the clergy shape the manners of a nation, but Mary does not believe it. Edmund responds:

> "With regard to their influencing public manners, Miss Crawford must misunderstand me, or suppose I mean to call them the arbiters of good breeding, the regulators of refinement and courtesy, the masters of the ceremonies of life. The manners I speak of, might rather be called conduct, perhaps, the result of good principle."

With regard to "refinement and courtesy," the Crawfords are without equal in the book. But that does not mean they conduct themselves according to good principles, which is the true meaning of "good manners." Fanny's comments elsewhere on the variety of nature apply here: It is wondrous that the same (English) soil and the same sun should produce "plants differing in the first rule and law of their existence." The first rule of existence for the Crawfords is quite different from that of the other characters.

This distinction between good breeding and good principles is developed and broadened in connection with two other main themes. As mentioned above, the first of these is acting. A central scene in the book is the home theatrical production that the young people plan during Sir Thomas's absence, over the objections of Edmund (at least initially) and Fanny. (This is one of the main charges against Fanny—she is a prude because she is so resolute in condemning a harmless entertainment. I shall return to this point below.) But the acting theme is pervasive. Henry is a natural actor on stage, and a public reader of considerable power. Even when Fanny is trying to resist his advances, she cannot help but be fascinated by his reading of a passage from Shakespeare. Henry is a wonderful actor because he is *always* acting. Fanny recognizes this from the beginning—he trifles, he flirts, at every moment he is playing a part—but, importantly, it is never the *same* part twice. That makes him charming, not least to many readers; but we as readers are supposed to be learning to see through his play-acting to search instead, as Fanny does, for strong principles and upright character, for some semblance of a permanent role beneath the Protean exterior.

The second related theme is a geographic one. Space almost plays the role of a character in the book. Not only do certain towns have important thematic associations, but the living space has a subtle influence on character. Fanny's life is divided between two locations. Early in the novel, she moves from her family's home in Portsmouth to live with her uncle and aunt Bertram at Mansfield Park. Her large family lived in cramped housing, and Fanny is at first overwhelmed by the size of everything at Mansfield:

> The grandeur of the house astonished, but could not console her. The rooms were too large for her to move in with ease; whatever she touched she expected to injure, and she crept about in constant terror of some-

> thing or other; often retreating towards her own chamber to cry; and the little girl who was spoken of in the drawing-room when she left at night, as seeming so desirably sensible of her peculiar good fortune, ended every day's sorrows by sobbing herself to sleep.

To make the Park a livable space, Fanny sets up a little "nest of comforts" in the East room, where she retreats to read and think. Even there, the fact that she is marginal to Mansfield Park is emphasized by the fact that Mrs. Norris allows no fire in the room.

Fanny eventually adjusts to the space of Mansfield, and this is most dramatically evident during her return trip to visit her family in Portsmouth in Book 3:

> Fanny was almost stunned. The smallness of the house, and the thinness of the walls, brought every thing so close to her, that, added to the fatigue of her journey, and all her recent agitation, she hardly knew how to bear it. *Within* the room all was tranquil enough, for Susan having disappeared with the others, there were soon only her father and herself remaining; and he taking out a newspaper—the accustomary loan of a neighbor, applied himself to studying it, without seeming to recollect her existence. The solitary candle was held between himself and the paper, without any reference to her possible convenience; but she had nothing to do, and was glad to have the light screened from her aching head, as she sat in bewildered, broken, sorrowful contemplation. She was at home.

Space may be cramped, but she is as distant from everyone as she ever was as a child at Mansfield. The only light is the candle held by her father, and she is screened from it by her father's newspaper. Instead of creating a circle of light in which two might sit, the light illumines only one.

Fanny's story is symbolized by this move from Portsmouth to Mansfield and back. She comes from the chaos and disorderliness of Portsmouth, and is formed into a young woman by Mansfield. Mansfield has the classic English virtues of repose, quietness, and stoic endurance. It is a country place in contrast to the bustling port city of Portsmouth. It takes the raw material of a Portsmouth and transforms it into a noble woman. The influence of place on character and even appearance is highlighted by Fanny's contemplation of her mother's looks during their walk to church:

> Her poor mother now did not look so very unworthy
> of being Lady Bertram's sister as she was but too apt
> to look. It often grieved her to the heart—to think
> of the contrast between them—to think that where
> nature had made so little difference, circumstances
> should have made so much, and that her mother, as
> handsome as Lady Bertram, and some years her junior,
> should have an appearance so much more worn and
> faded, so comfortless, so slatternly, so shabby.

That was Fanny's future, but for the intervention of Mansfield Park. To this extent, the novel could be seen as a celebration of the values of the English nobility.

But all is not well at the Park either, and that is so largely because a third location is also thematically significant—London. Henry and Mary Crawford come to Mansfield Park from London, and bring London with them. London is the maker of manners, the Hollywood of early-nineteenth-century England, the pacesetter for all things fashionable—or so the Crawfords think. Mary cannot wait to get back to London, but in the meantime, she and her brother help to set up an outpost of London manners at Mansfield. The Crawfords desire for entertainment, their need for amusement, their impatience with old ways, and their eagerness always to be attempting some novelty infects the rest of the young people at Mansfield Park. Henry agrees to act because it is among those pleasures he has never had, and he talks persistently about "improvements" at Rushworth's Sotherton and even at Edmund's parish home in Thornton Lacey. London is a city of actors, full of people who, having no settled place in life, are constantly trying on some new role. One dimension of the conflict of the novel lies here: Who is to be the maker of manners? London? Or the Church?

Individualism arises from the detachment of breeding from true manners—symbolized by acting and by the influence of London values on the wealthy inhabitants of the Park. One of the most profound aspects of Austen's novel is her rich and detailed depiction of two perfect individualists. Henry is thought plain by everyone, until his charming and flirtatious ways, as well as his large income, begin to inflame Maria's and Julia's imagination. Only Fanny remains convinced that he is quite plain. Mary is pretty and lively, and shows an immediate interest in Tom Bertram, though she shortly shifts attention to his brother Edmund. Henry's manners are so good that Mrs. Grant, his sister, imputes to him all other good qualities, and, though initially finding him "plain and black," the Bertram sisters are so taken by his manners that they decide that he is exceedingly good-looking. "Manners" here should be taken in the sense of flirtatious attentions, which Henry bestows in great measure. Henry's "manners" in one sense are bad: He does not conduct himself well. But he is so adept at playing social roles that his manners in another sense please everyone—everyone but the perceptive Fanny, who takes time to look and think.

Henry's behavior does not flow from or produce order and

decorum; on the contrary, his conduct leads to continuous upheaval and chaos. Though elegant and rich, he is a Satan, who delights in the chaos that he causes. It is not merely that he has no "fixed role" and no "calling"; he refuses to recognize the "fixed fate" of others, and attempts to seduce them from their vocations. During one of his early conversations with his sister, he says that he prefers the engaged Maria Bertram to her younger sister Julia:

> "An engaged woman is always more agreeable than a disengaged. She is satisfied with herself. Her cares are over, and she feels that she may exert all her powers of pleasing without suspicion. All is safe with a lady engaged; no harm can be done."

This turns the purpose of an engagement upside down; engagement does not free the engaged woman to flirt without suspicion, but limits her relations with other men. Henry would turn engagement into disengagement.

Henry's delight in chaos is even more explicit later, when he reflects on the fun the young people all had planning the play:

> "I shall always look back on our theatricals with exquisite pleasure. There was such an interest, such an animation, such a spirit diffused! Everybody felt it. We were all alive. There was employment, hope, solicitude, bustle, for every hour of the day. Always some little objection, some little doubt, some little anxiety to be got over. I never was happier."

Fanny silently condemns him: "Never happier than when behaving so dishonorably and unfeelingly!—Oh! what a corrupted mind!"

Another important dimension of Henry's individualism is evident in a conversation later in the book, which significantly takes place during a game of "speculation." Sir Thomas first begins to discern Henry's attention to Fanny, and speculates about their future relationship; Fanny speculates about life at Mansfield after Edmund has left to take up his pastoral charge at Thornton Lacey; and Henry indulges in speculations of his own, mainly about the "improvements" that could be made to Edmund's future home. Edmund will be satisfied to give the home "the air of a gentleman's residence," but Henry is not content with such minimal improvements:

> "You may raise it into a *place*. From being the mere gentleman's residence, it becomes, by judicious improvement, the residence of a man of education, taste, modern manners, good connections. All this may be stamped on it; and that house receive such an air as to make its own be set down as a great land-holder of the parish, by every creature traveling the road."

Henry is still insisting on "improvements" that would make Edmund's pastoral home into something other than it is. More than that, Henry is still conspiring with his sister, in this case not to snare Fanny but to snare Edmund. While Henry speaks, Mary has been speculating about going with Edmund to his new home, but is shocked when she is "no longer able, in the picture she had been forming of a future Thornton, to shut out the church, sink the clergyman, and see only the respectable, elegant, modernized, and occasional residence of a man of independent fortune." Henry and Mary are interested in the parish home at Thornton only so long as they can remove the parish.

Even after he has declared his intention to settle down and marry Fanny, Henry does not grasp the significance of that decision. This point is again made in a conversation dealing with Edmund's calling. After Henry has read a passage from Shakespeare to good effect, he and Edmund discuss the importance of clerical reading. Edmund agrees that "distinctness and energy" in reading "may have weight in recommending the most solid truths." But Henry's treatment of the subject reduces liturgical reading and preaching to another form of acting:

> "A sermon, well delivered, is more uncommon even than prayers well read. A sermon, good in itself, is no rare thing. It is more difficult to speak well than to compose well; that is, the rules and tricks of composition are oftener an object of study. A thoroughly good sermon, thoroughly well delivered, is a capital gratification. I can never hear such a one without the greatest admiration and respect, and more than half a mind to take orders and preach myself. There is something in the eloquence of the pulpit, when it is really eloquence, which is entitled to the highest praise and honor."

Sermonizing is another "role" that Henry would dearly love to play (since it would be new), so long as he could preach only to educated congregations. And not too often: Preaching occasionally would suit, but "not for a constancy; it would not do for a constancy." But constancy, perseverance, a long obedience in one direction—this, of course, is precisely the difference between acting a role and accepting a role as a vocation. When Henry realizes that Fanny has noted his objection to "constancy," Fanny replies: "I thought it a pity you did not always know yourself as well as you seemed to do at that moment." Henry is addicted to novelty and will try anything new because it is new.

Mary Crawford is the female version of her brother, an actress and opportunist. Her character is established in part by contrast with Fanny. One particularly striking example is found in Book 2 (chapter 22), during a conversation in which Fanny rhapsodizes on the beauties of evergreens. Fanny is commenting on the wonderful changes that have taken place in the grounds at Mansfield Park, and this leads her into an astonished meditation on memory:

> "How wonderful, how very wonderful the operations of time, and the changes of the human mind! . . . If any one faculty of our nature may be called *more* wonderful than the rest, I do think it is memory. There seems something more speakingly incomprehensible in the powers, the failures, the inequalities of memory, than in any other of our intelligences. The memory is sometimes so retentive, so serviceable, so obedient—at others, so bewildered and so weak—and at others again, so tyrannic, so beyond control!—we are to be sure a miracle every way—but our powers of recollecting and of forgetting, do seem peculiarly past finding out."

This is a striking statement in many ways: it is a celebration of memory worthy of Augustine, whose *Confessions* remains the classic on the subject. The "past finding out" is clearly a biblical or liturgical reference that indicates that Fanny is attributing the mystery of memory to God. But the most striking thing about this statement is Mary's reaction: "Miss Crawford, untouched and inattentive, had nothing to say." Not only does Mary have no sense of the beauty of the creation or the wonders of the human mind. She simply has no memory; she is all and always new. An actor needs no memory of a past, since he can always adopt a new past at will; an individualist wants no past, since having a past would limit his choice of new roles in the present.

The Crawfords are also individualists in another, more subtle, but profound sense. In all her novels, Austen displays her assumption that moral life is always lived in community. We need others to guide and teach us, and several of Austen's novels hinge on the ability of a woman to find a suitable mentor (Emma finds Knightley, Catherine Morland finds Henry Tilney). Living in community also means recognizing that our actions are not our own, but always affect others. In the *Nicomachean Ethics*, Aristotle distinguished between different sorts of action on the basis of what they produce outside the actors:

> Production (*poesis*) is different from action (*praxis*)...
> and so the reasoned state that is capable of action is also
> different from that which is capable of production.
> Hence neither is included in the other; because action
> is not production, nor production action.

Though this seems innocent, it has tremendously broad implications. For Aristotle, ethics deals with action and not with production, and this means that the whole realm of arts and economic activity is outside the strict boundaries of the ethical. But the distinction rests on a fundamental mistake—namely, that our actions can be confined to ourselves, that we can engage in *praxis* without producing *anything* outside ourselves. However Aristotelian Austen was in other respects, she implicitly rejects Aristotle's distinction between *praxis* (actions whose effects remain with the actor) and *poesis* (actions whose effects go beyond the actor), for she knows that every action is "poetic."

Henry and Mary Crawford do not recognize the inherent poetry of life. They are individualists in the sense that they follow their own desires regardless of what authorities say or do. When Sir Thomas is away on business, they take part in a theatrical production, and in fact press for it, even though they are warned that the master of the house would disapprove, and even over the initial objections of Edmund, who is responsible for managing the house in his father's absence. More subtly, they have no sense that their actions have consequences beyond the individual. When Henry runs away with Maria, now

Mrs. Rushworth, Mary Crawford is still hoping that Edmund will want to marry her. She is utterly insensible to the fact that Henry's scandal might affect *her* in any way.

This brings us to what is perhaps the central critical judgment against *Mansfield Park*—Fanny Price. In Whit Stillman's intriguingly Austenesque film, *Metropolitan*, Tom Townsend, the young man from across town who has been befriended by the group of debutantes and preppies, is astonished when Audrey Rouget, the leading female character, reveals that she enjoys *Mansfield Park*. Everyone knows, Tom says, that *Mansfield Park* is the worst novel Jane Austen wrote, and nobody likes the book's heroine, Fanny Price. Audrey, the moral center of the film and very much a Fanny Price character herself, protests simply, "I like Fanny Price." It is later revealed that Tom has never read *Mansfield Park*, or anything else by Jane Austen for that matter. He prefers to read critics. At Audrey's urging, Tom eventually reads some Austen and is delighted with it.

Tom certainly had his choice of critics to support his hostility to *Mansfield Park* and Fanny Price. To be sure, *Mansfield Park* has not always been as sharply criticized as it is today. During Austen's lifetime, it vied with *Pride and Prejudice* as Austen's best-loved novel. Even today, Tony Tanner perceptively (and, in my judgment, accurately) calls *Mansfield Park* one of the "most profound novels" of the nineteenth century. Yet the novel, and its heroine, have endured sharp attacks. Lord David Cecil said that Fanny was "a little wooden, a little charmless, and rather a prig." Kingsley Amis was vicious: Fanny is "a monster of complacency and pride." Another saw her as "the most terrible incarnation we have of the female prig-pharisee," and C. S. Lewis found little to admire: Fanny has "nothing except rectitude of mind; neither passion, nor physical courage, nor wit, nor resource." Others have suggested that Fanny makes a fatal mistake in rejecting the vivacious, interesting, and very rich Henry Crawford in favor of the dull and stiff clergyman Edmund Bertram.

These attacks on Fanny show that their authors are as incapable of seeing her qualities as Mrs. Norris is, and indeed incapable of following Austen's clear directions for judging Fanny. It is often pointed out that of all of Austen's heroines, Fanny is one of only two (Anne Elliot is the other) who is not treated with irony, who does not make any serious misjudgment, whose behavior is always supported by the narrator. Elizabeth Bennet willfully misjudges Darcy, Emma misjudges everything, Catherine Morland is for most of *Northanger Abbey* too ignorant to form judgments, and even the sensible Elinor Dashwood collects enough mistakes to fill a small cupboard. Unless we are to suspect Austen of a hyper-ironic stance where Austen's lack of irony toward Fanny is a way of reinforcing irony, then we should accept at face value that Austen considers Fanny morally and intellectually exemplary.

To be sure, Fanny—physically weak, easily fatigued, often painfully shy and backward, with little wit—suffers in many respects by comparison to the other characters in the book. She is indeed an unusual heroine. Mary Crawford is thoroughly her brother's sister, full of wit and life and sparkle, a secular angel who charms Edmund Bertram by playing the harp. Julia and Maria Bertram, Edmund's sisters, are more accomplished than Fanny. Of the male characters, Edmund is surely the least immediately attractive. Not only Henry, but Tom Bertram, Edmund's wastrel older brother, and John Yates, the fervent actor, seem more interesting. Rushworth, who marries Maria, is a dolt cut from the same cloth as Mr. Collins in *Pride and Prejudice*, but his very doltishness makes him fun to read about.

In such a company, Edmund and Fanny are definitely not the standouts.

Yet given Austen's clear signals that they are the most moral and the central characters in the book, we have to say that this contrast is deliberate, and, further, that critics who side with the Crawfords against Edmund and Fanny are falling into the same trap as those Blakean critics who think that Milton was on the devil's side without knowing it. No doubt other characters are more immediately and superficially brilliant—but that is just the point. Austen wants our judgments about her characters to be shaped by the *principles* they display, not by their ability to charm. Charm deceives, and many are the critics who are taken in by it. Fanny's weakness and immobility are also part of the point. She shares much with classic Christian heroines like Constance in Chaucer's "Man of Law's Tale," who are heroines of *perseverance*. When Fanny refuses to marry Henry, these are precisely the issues in play. She distrusts Henry's character and his principles, and her heart is already committed to Edmund. Consistent with this perseverance, Fanny spends much of the novel in a single location, Mansfield Park, while many of the other characters come and go, and in several scenes, Fanny sits in the center of a swirl of activity. This is not a fault. Her very *immobility*, her stillness in a world running after vanity, makes her a heroine. She has a fixed fate, and she accepts it with gratitude. As she says during the controversy over the theatrical production, "I cannot act." She is a still point in a turning world.

Edmund Bertram is also a man with a "fixed fate," an assigned role. He is destined to be a clergyman, much to the astonishment of Mary Crawford, who thinks that clergymen are "nothing." Several of the key conversations in the novel are concerned with the issue of calling, the role of the clergy in the nation, and the contrast between the clergy of London and the clergy in the rest of England. The quotation from Edmund above is part of his defense of the indispensability of the Church for the health of the nation, and the illness that the upper classes of the novel are suffering is symbolized by the neglected and vacant chapel at Rushworth's Sotherton. Mary expresses the modern secularist mind-set: When told that morning prayers have been discontinued at Sotherton, she smiles and says, "Every generation has its improvements." Improvements again!

Edmund's calling lends an almost allegorical tone to the story. Edmund, the future guardian of morals, is attracted to the flashy novelty of Mary Crawford of London, and fails for some time to see her true character. Choosing this temptress would lead him far from his calling and, because the clergy are the protectors of morals, would contribute by omission to the decline of English morals. Eventually, however, he chooses the modest and moral Fanny Price. He is set up to choose between Lady Wisdom and Lady Folly, between the true Church and the false. (If there is a meta-irony in *Mansfield Park*, it is not that Austen secretly mocks Fanny; it is rather that Austen, the ironist, the realist, the literalist, is in the end Bunyan's blood-sister.)

As noted above, when Austen talked about the purpose and theme of *Mansfield Park*, she said she was writing on the subject of ordination, with the related themes of vocation or calling. That referred of course to Edmund's calling to be a clergyman and the temptation to abandon that vocation when Mary appears. The challenge before Edmund is to persevere in the role that he has been ordained to fill, and to resist the temptation to become an actor-individualist. And this is the same temptation that confronts Fanny. She has been "ordained" to love Edmund, and she must persevere through persistent temptations from Henry Crawford. Austen brings the two "vocations" of marriage and ordination into direct connection. While everyone is eagerly awaiting the Mansfield ball, Edmund has his mind on other things, being "deeply occupied in the consideration of the two important events now at hand, which were to fix his fate in life—ordination and matrimony." If there is allegory here, it cuts both ways: Not only must the shepherd resist the allurements of the false woman, but the bride must resist the advances of a charming but ultimately scurrilous suitor. Both must be faithful to their "fixed fates," unmoved by tempter or temptress.

"Vocation" is set in direct contrast to "acting." Both have to do with taking on or playing "roles," but the meaning of "role" in the two cases is quite different. An actor might adopt many different roles, none of which defines who he is. Actors have no "fixed fate" in life. Thus, in contrast to the "actors" of the story, Edmund is "called" to a particular "vocation." Though, as he emphasizes to Mary, he has chosen to pursue the ministry, in a more profound sense he has been chosen. And his role is determined not by the whims of the moment but by assuming a particular position within English society, a position established by the ritual of ordination, which determines the role he is going to play. He is not free to choose another "role" tomorrow. For a called man or woman, his or her role is not a mask that can be removed at will. The mask sticks so closely to his face as to be permanent. The health of Mansfield, of England, depends on which path is chosen, on whether the next generation chooses to be "actors" or to accept "ordination."

Both Fanny and Edmund are tempted to give up their "fixed fates" and become "actors," and this is symbolized by their day at Sotherton. The geography of the walk at Sotherton is important. The immediate grounds of the house are bounded by a wall and a gate, and then the "wilderness," a wooded and wilder area. During this walk in the "wilderness," Miss Crawford attempts to dissuade Edmund about his clerical calling. It is a kind of temptation scene, in a garden-wilderness, with Mary herself as the forbidden fruit. Austen adds another touch to indicate just how dangerous a position Edmund is in: The entire conversation takes place off the "great path" in the "serpentine" path of the wilderness walk. Edmund is tempted to give up his clerical "role" for another; he is tempted to become an actor, to leave the great path that is fated for him.

The denouement of the book comes through a series of letters, which completely unveil the Crawfords as the unthinking individualists that they are. When Tom Bertram becomes seriously ill, Mary writes to express the hope that the Bertram fortune will now fall into Edmund's more deserving possession. She is willing to accept a clergyman husband, so long as he is sufficiently wealthy and potentially stylish. Even when Henry runs away with Maria Rushworth, Mary thinks that there is no barrier to her continuing connection with Edmund. Mary describes Henry and Maria as "foolish," and the mildness of that judgment offends Edmund: "No harsher name than folly given—so voluntarily, so freely, so coolly to canvass it!—no reluctance, no horror, no feminine—shall I say? no modest loathings!—This is what the world does." Newly ordained pastor that he is, Edmund is surely using "world" in its fullest biblical sense; worldliness leads only to disaster.

The tour at Sotherton is also important for seeing how Austen diagnoses the ills at Mansfield Park, for seeing how Austen treats the sources of disruptive individualism. As Maria says with pride, the town church is well situated at a distance from the house: "The church spire is reckoned remarkably handsome. I am glad the church is not so close to the Great House as often happens in old places. The annoyance of the bells must be terrible." The church is acknowledged only for its contribution to the aesthetics of the town; so long as it does not intrude too closely on the life of the Great House, all is well. Every generation has its improvements, as Mary might say. Similarly, the chapel is remarkable for being "fitted up as you see it, in James the Second's time," and because at one time "the linings and cushions of the pulpit and family-seat were only purple cloth." In short, "it is a handsome chapel." And that is all.

It is in this chapel that the first conversation about clerical office begins. Fanny believes that a family at regular prayer is part of "what such a household should be," but Mary disagrees: "It is safer to leave people to their own devices on such subjects." Even in politics, Mary is an individualist, defending liberty of conscience in religious matters. She is shocked, then, to learn that Edmund intends to be ordained, and even more shocked that he should have *chosen* the Church as a profession: "A clergyman is nothing," she says, referring to his social standing. Edmund gives a spirited defense of the essential place of the clergy in the nation:

> "A clergyman cannot be high in state or fashion. He must not head mobs, or set the tone in dress. But I cannot call that situation nothing, which has the charge of all that is of the first importance to mankind, individually or collectively considered, temporally and eternally—which has the guardianship of religion and morals, and consequently the manners which result from their influence. No one here can call the *office* nothing. If the man who holds it is so, it is by the neglect of his duty, by forgoing its just importance, and stepping out of his place to appear what he ought

not to appear."

Mary cannot believe that the clergy have such weight, since one sees any of them "so rarely out of his pulpit." But here the contrast of London and the rest of England comes into play, as Edmund insists that a proper clergyman is not merely a pulpiteer:

> "A fine preacher is followed and admired; but it is not in fine preaching only that a good clergyman will be useful in his parish and his neighborhood, where the parish and neighborhood are of a size capable of knowing his private character, and observing his general conduct, which in London can rarely be the case."

Several things are happening in this conversation. Clearly, Austen's sympathies are with Edmund, who speaks in tones not unlike his great namesake, Edmund Burke. Edmund's choice is for a high calling, one that does indeed direct the manners and conduct of the nation. Sotherton is "improving," and closing the chapel is one of these improvements. But a house so improved is destined to fall, and Sotherton will fall resoundingly before the end of the novel. Moreover, Mary's worldliness, her sense of being on the cutting edge of social evolution, is undercut here with sharp irony. She believes that in knowing London she knows the world: "The metropolis, I imagine, is a pretty fair sample of the rest," and that means if a clergyman is nothing in London he is nothing anywhere. On the contrary, Edmund argues, London is a very small and very special world; knowing London does not give Mary knowledge of the world. It is provincial and parochial. Especially here, the thematic conflict of the novel takes center stage: London versus the Church.

Of course, the perversion of the nobility at Mansfield Park is not altogether London's fault. Even before Henry and Mary arrive, it is clear that something is amiss. Good breeding and good conduct have already been separated, as Sir Thomas has singularly failed to pass on his own sense of propriety and morals to his children. Maria and Julia are well educated "in everything but disposition," and though they mock Fanny for not knowing the "principal rivers in Russia," they are "entirely deficient in the less common acquirements of self-knowledge, generosity, and humility," all subjects in which Fanny excels. Tom, the eldest Bertram, is even worse, a ne'er-do-well who has none of his father's sense of responsibility for the moral climate of the Bertram house or for the repute of the Bertram name. In part, Austen is focusing attention on the collapsing morals of the upper classes of England. *Mansfield Park*'s cast of characters is socially much higher than the characters in Austen's other novels. Henry and Mary have been exceedingly rich for some years, Rushworth has £12,000, the Bertrams have no monetary wants or cares. Put energetic young people in a house, remove adult restraint, stir in vast sums of money: that, Austen thinks, is a recipe for trouble.

Sir Thomas recognizes too that "this is what the world does." He recognizes the failures of his parenting of his daughters:

> Something had been wanting *within*, or time would have worn away much of its ill effect. He feared that principle, active principle, had been wanting, that they had never been properly taught to govern their inclinations and tempers, by that sense of duty which can alone suffice. They had been instructed theoretically in their religion, but never required to bring it into daily practice.

Like the Rushworth family, Sir Thomas had, symbolically if not in fact, discontinued the prayers that make a house, and left the chapel disused and empty. Without a guardian, without a pastor or guide, his daughters had fallen in with "how the world goes."

Nearly seduced by the world, nearly led astray by the world to abandon his vocation and become a mere actor, Edmund in the end accepts his calling. "I cannot act," Fanny says, and indeed she cannot, and neither can Edmund. In the end, they both accept, gratefully, their ordained roles, their "fixed fate."

Austen was not an unthinking defender of traditional social order. Not uncommonly, her heroines are upwardly mobile, particularly through the agency of matrimony. Yet she sensed the corrosive effects of individualism, and her uncanny intelligence and attention to the details of social surface enabled her to give us one of literature's sharpest portraits of this emerging reality. That she also recognized the absence and failure of the Church in combating this decay makes her a public theologian to reckon with.

8   The Witness of Czesław Miłosz

JEREMY DRISCOLL, November 2004

C ZESŁAW Miłosz was born in Szetejnie in 1911 and raised in Wilno, both of which are in present-day Lithuania. His family was part of the large Polish-speaking population of that city. For this reason he identified himself as a Polish writer. Living there through his university education, he was present in 1939 when the Soviets invaded Lithuania, while Hitler simultaneously invaded Poland. At great personal risk, he escaped through the Soviet borders and worked for the Polish resistance in Warsaw throughout the war. Once the war had ended, he tried to make a life for himself in his own nation and was part of the diplomatic corps of Communist Poland's postwar government. He was posted to the consulate in New York and the embassy in Washington. In 1951, while he was serving as the cultural attaché at the Polish embassy in Paris, he defected. He remained in France until 1960, when he took a position at the University of California, Berkeley, as a professor of Slavic literature. In 1980, at the age of seventy, he received the Nobel Prize for Literature. Having lived in exile for fifty years, he moved from the United States to Krakow in 2001 and died there in 2004 at the age of ninety-three. He had remained productive until the end; a final book of poems, *Second Space,* was published in English in the fall of 2004.

This bare-bones summary of his life shows that Miłosz's personal history included almost the whole of the twentieth century. He participated in some of its most dramatic episodes and lived within several of its colliding cultures, carving out homes in Lithuania, Poland, France, and the United States. These are the contexts in which his Christian vision was shaped and delivered. Although he often expressed this vision obliquely, he was relentless in his criticism of those who despised faith as an anachronism:

> I am not afraid to say that a devout and God-fearing man is superior as a human specimen to a restless mocker who is glad to style himself an 'intellectual,' proud of his cleverness in using ideas which he claims as his own though he acquired them in a pawnshop in exchange for simplicity of heart . . . . The sacred exists and is stronger than all our rebellions.

Miłosz believed that the role of the poet is crucial in any society—regardless of how little poetry is appreciated or its importance understood. Consider his apologia for the poetry he was writing during and after World War II, when the world was undergoing a shock and disillusionment perhaps unparalleled in human history. How should the poet react? Here is Miłosz's proposal:

> As is well known, the philosopher Adorno said that it would be an abomination to write lyric poetry after Auschwitz, and the philosopher Emmanuel Levinas gave the year 1941 as the date when God "abandoned" us. Whereas I wrote idyllic verses, "The World" and a number of others, in the very center of what was taking place in the *anus mundi*, and not by any means out of ignorance. . . . Life does not like death. The

body, as long as it is able to, sets in opposition to death
the heart's contractions and the warmth of circulating
blood. Gentle verses written in the midst of horror
declare themselves for life; they are the body's rebellion
against its destruction.

To retain simplicity of heart, to write verses for life against
death—these gentle-sounding goals are not achieved without
cost or without a sustaining faith. Yet here it is necessary to
remind ourselves of the paradoxical way in which faith is practiced. Faith is practiced in the struggle with faith. Miłosz had
the courage to expose his struggle in all its intensity; thus the
readers with whom he shared his troubles and doubts can trust,
or at least consider with appropriate seriousness, his decision
to stand within faith's orbit. In a 1959 letter to the Catholic
monk and writer Thomas Merton, Miłosz wrote,

> As to my Catholicism, this is perhaps a subject for a
> whole letter. In any case few people suspect my basi-
> cally religious interests and I have never been ranged
> among 'Catholic writers.' Which, strategically, is per-
> haps better. We are obliged to bear witness. But of
> what? That we pray to have faith? This problem—
> how much we should say openly—is always present
> in my thoughts.

Two things stand out in this candid letter. First, his careful consideration of how best to treat religious themes in his writing.
Second, the depth of his humility and poverty before faith.

In one poem, he addresses God wryly, saying, "It seems to
me that people who cannot believe in you / deserve your praise,"
and he confesses later in the same poem, "I pray to you, for I do
not know how not to pray." This struggle spanned his entire
life. Only a few years ago, feeling his age, he wrote,

> Now You are closing down my five senses, slowly,

And I am an old man lying in darkness . . .
Liberate me from guilt, real and imagined.
Give me certainty that I toiled for Your glory.
In the hour of the agony of death, help me with Your
suffering
Which cannot save the world from pain.

In a piece written in 1991 he mused at length about the difficulty of sharing thoughts like these.

I feel obliged to speak the truth to my contemporaries
and I feel ashamed if they take me to be someone who
I am not. In their opinion, a person who 'had faith' is
fortunate. They assume that as a result of certain inner
experiences he was able to find an answer, while they
know only questions. So how can I make a profession
of faith in the presence of my fellow human beings?
After all, I am one of them, seeking, as they do, the
laws of inheritance, and I am just as confused. . . .

But let us come to the content of what he believed:

To put it very simply and bluntly, I must ask if I believe
that the four Gospels tell the truth. My answer to this
is: Yes. So I believe in an absurdity, that Jesus rose from
the dead? Just answer without any of those evasions
and artful tricks employed by theologians: Yes or No?
I answer: Yes, and by that response I nullify death's
omnipotence. If I am mistaken in my faith, I offer it
as a challenge to the Spirit of the Earth. . . .

Later in the same piece he asked,

Ought I to try to explain "why I believe"? I don't think
so. It should suffice if I attempt to convey the coloring
or tone. If I believed that man can do good with his
own powers, I would have no interest in Christianity.
But he cannot, because he is enslaved to his own preda-
tory, domineering instincts. . . . Evil grows and bears

> fruit, which is understandable, because it has logic and
> probability on its side and also, of course, strength.
> The resistance of tiny kernels of good, to which no
> one grants the power of causing far-reaching conse-
> quences, is entirely mysterious, however. Such seem-
> ing nothingness not only lasts but contains within
> itself enormous energy which is revealed gradually.
> One can draw momentous conclusions from this.

Miłosz believed that the religious question ought to be explored
in the mainstream of literature and culture. As he grew older,
he used the authority he had acquired to challenge those of
his colleagues who believed that discussions of religion were
beneath their dignity. "To write on literature or art was considered an honorable occupation," he wrote in 1997,

> whereas any time notions taken from the language
> of religion appeared, the one who brought them up
> was immediately treated as lacking in tact, as if a silent
> pact had been broken. Yet I lived at a time when a
> huge change in the contents of the human imagina-
> tion was occurring. In my lifetime Heaven and Hell
> disappeared, the belief in life after death was consider-
> ably weakened. How could I not think of this? And
> is it not surprising that my preoccupation was a rare
> case?

Czesław Miłosz stood apart as a poet who dared to be preoccupied with such things. He believed that many of the horrors of
the twentieth century had their roots in the effort to liberate
people from religion. Miłosz witnessed these efforts first-hand
and reflected on their results:

> Religion, opium for the people. To those suffering
> pain, humiliation, illness, and serfdom, it promised a
> reward in an afterlife. And now we are witnessing a
> transformation. A true opium for the people is a belief

> in nothingness after death—the huge solace of think-
> ing that for our betrayals, greed, cowardice, murder
> we are not going to be judged.

The evidence of Miłosz's Christianity is spread throughout his poems and essays in fragmentary clues. Rarely did he discuss the topic systematically. His faith was often a kind of secret which, once noticed, could explain at least in part his choice of themes and subjects. But sometimes it would come to the surface of his work. In 2002, Miłosz published a long poem that was meant to function as a testimonial, *A Theological Treatise*. Miłosz was aware that he was risking his reputation by venturing to write about theology, but he chose to use his credibility and clout to address a theme that literary fashion silently prohibited. "Why theology?" he asks in the first paragraph of this poem. (There are twenty-three paragraphs in the whole treatise, each containing varying numbers of stanzas.) He answers, "Because the first must be first. / And first is a notion of truth." The paragraph concludes with a plea and a stipulation: "Let reality return to our speech. / That is, meaning. Impossible without an absolute point of reference." In this testimonial poem, Miłosz directly acknowledges God as the absolute point of reference. Many of the Christian themes scattered throughout his writings are here gathered together. One such theme is the frank expression of his own struggle with various elements of Catholic life. He always took theology seriously, but he sometimes wrote about theologians with bitter irony. He found the clericalism in some sectors of the Polish Church to be exaggerated and distasteful.

> I apologize, most reverend theologians, for a tone
>   not befitting
> the purple of your robes.
> I thrash in the bed of my style, searching for a

> comfortable position,
> not too sanctimonious, not too mundane.
> There must be a middle place between abstrac-
>   tion and childishness
> where one can talk seriously about serious things.

Miłosz was wary of the comfortable abstract formulas offered by the academic theologian; they seemed to have little to
do with the horrible questions his life story had forced him to
confront. He recoiled from mechanical presentations of doctrine and easy explanations of suffering. When a clerical and
theological style becomes stiff or sanctimonious, it cannot be
taken seriously by people engaged in life-and-death struggles.
But a poetry that spoke only of this-worldly things—a poetry
that was "too mundane"—would fail to satisfy the deepest
longings of the heart. Miłosz rightly aims for a "middle place"
where it is possible to "talk seriously about serious things."

Yet Miłosz believed, somewhat problematically, that the
most serious things resisted any kind of definition. The mysteries of the faith were to be praised, described, but not explained.
"Catholic dogmas are a few inches too high; we stand on our
toes / and for a moment it seems to us that we see," he writes in
the *Treatise*. "Yet the mystery of the Holy Trinity, the mystery
of Original Sin, / the mystery of the Redemption are all well
armored against reason . . . / What in all that can be grasped
by little girls dressed in white for First Communion?"

Miłosz's long testimonial poem also reveals his gnostic lean-
ings. The tendency makes for interesting poems, but it adds
to his difficulties with Catholic theology. "Not out of frivolity,
most reverend theologians, I busied myself with the secret /
knowledge of many centuries, but out of the pain in my heart
when I looked out / at the atrocity of the world." Here Miłosz
is explaining and justifying his turn to gnostic texts for help.

He addresses himself to the "most reverend theologians" to complain that his need was not being met by their pat assurances. The pain Miłosz refers to in this poem is not merely an intellectual sorrow: he is writing not just about the universal tragedy; he is writing about the tragedies of his own life. Wounded by the betrayals and injustices he has witnessed, he longs to understand the mysteries of evil and innocent suffering: "If God is all-powerful, he can allow all this only if he is not good. / Wherefrom then the limits of his power? Why such an order of creation? They all / tried to find an answer, heretics, kabbalists, alchemists, the Knights of the Rose Cross." Here he cites the gnostic sources to which he turned. Surely he was led in this direction by reading Jacob Boehme, who had so strongly influenced Adam Mickiewicz, the critical point of reference for all modern Polish poetry.

It would have been impossible for Miłosz not to have gone this gnostic way, at least to some extent. In addition to the Mickiewicz influence, his own temperament inclined him toward it. The horrors he lived through caused him to pose the same questions as these gnostic texts, and orthodox Christianity was not giving him the spiritual answers he needed. But if the Christianity of his time and place was not delivering those answers, this does not mean that the answers were not there. And in Miłosz's struggle we see him betray an instinctive understanding that this may be the case. This explains why, in the midst of the *Treatise*'s lengthy discussion of gnostic questions, he also narrates his own practice of Catholic life. He is being driven by something larger than himself, and it is nothing less than his whole Catholic faith, whether he always chooses it or not. He admits, "Alas, an American saying has applied to me, though it was not coined with kindly intent: / 'Once a Catholic, always a Catholic.'" He is not always comfortable with his religious inheritance, and yet something compels him never to abandon it.

Miłosz often sensed a lack in his own faith, and he confesses this in the *Treatise*, as elsewhere (e.g., "Distance"): "Why not concede," he asks, "that I have not progressed, in my religion, / past the Book of Job?" This can best be understood in light of something he tells us later in the poem: "Only a dark tone, an inclination toward a peculiar Manichean / strain of Christianity, could have led one to the proper trail." Here "the proper trail" means the proper interpretation of his work. All this comes in the paragraph that begins, "To present myself at last as an heir to mystical lodges . . ." He is confessing much, disclosing much, at these points in his testament. He is providing his readers with clearer information about his spiritual life. Hence the "at last" which introduces this revealing paragraph. He is expressing relief as he finally reveals the sources and limits of his religious anxiety.

What is significant for Miłosz's readers in this kind of writing is that he names in himself what is a fundamental religious question of our times; namely, getting past Job. Getting past Job—or for that matter, getting past a Manichean Christianity—is a serious religious challenge. The Christian tradition is in fact equipped to take the serious searcher past Job, but it was precisely this part of the tradition that was somehow not delivered to Miłosz and which does not appear in the poem. I would suggest that it is only possible to move past Job by going through Job.

There is a tradition of Christian exegesis which reads Job as a prophecy of Christ. One can even imagine Job's complaint provoking the Incarnation and the cross as the response from God. The prefiguration becomes explicit at Job 10:4–5, where Job says to God, "Have you eyes of flesh? Do you see as man sees? Are your days as the days of a mortal?" In fact, in the Incarnation and the death of Jesus, God can now answer Yes to this question. This Yes is strongly underlined in the phrase from St. Paul in the Letter to the Philippians 2:8: "obedient unto death, yes, death on a cross." In the same part of the poem where Miłosz quipped about the little girls dressed in white for First Communion, he also warns, "And it will not do to prattle on about sweet little Jesus / in the hay of his cradle." But, of course, sweet little Jesus in the hay is not the central announcement of Christian faith. The central announcement is Jesus Christ, "and him crucified" (1 Corinthians 2:2). Miłosz's warning against a sweet little Jesus is equivalent to Job's demand for a serious answer to his serious question. But the death of Jesus on the cross is God's serious answer. In the end, Miłosz's *Treatise* does not grapple deeply enough with this divine answer.

To come back to Miłosz's words at this point in the poem, he notes a difference between himself and Job—namely, that Job thought of himself as innocent while the poet is not. "I was not innocent, I wanted to be innocent, but I couldn't be." But in the end it was not Job's innocence that was important but rather the majesty and mystery of God, before which Job bowed down and became silent. In an earlier writing Miłosz had shown himself to be aware that this was the key insight of Job, even if, in the poet's version of the story, God says things that are rather more severe than anything to be found in the book of Job. In a little essay titled "Misfortune" in *Miłosz's ABCs*, Miłosz writes, "To create a universe like the one we have is not nice. 'And why should I have to be nice?' asks God. 'Where did you get such ideas?' " This is strong thinking. It is acquiescence to the impenetrable mystery of God, an acquiescence to whatever of God the death of Jesus on the cross is meant to reveal.

When in the *Treatise* Miłosz refers to his own practices as a

Catholic, he speaks with a remarkable humility, contrasting his own weakness with the strength of the communion to which he belongs. This humility is especially striking since Miłosz was, by temperament, a proud man, as he himself often acknowledged. His fine mind and his natural sophistication caused him to hesitate before the requirements of faith. But in the end he rejected the option of turning his sophistication against more simple believers. Near the very beginning of the *Treatise* he states, "The opposition, I versus they, seemed immoral. / It meant he [Miłosz] considered himself better than they were." At the end, having agonized through much of the poem over the questions posed by his gnostic favorites, he comes back much more strongly to a defense of the categories of Christian worship. "Treat with understanding persons of weak faith. / Myself included," he writes.

> One day I believe, another I disbelieve.
> Yet I feel warmth among people at prayer.
> Since they believe, they help me to believe
> in their existence, these incomprehensible beings.
>
> · ·
>
> Naturally, I am a skeptic. Yet I sing with them,
> thus overcoming the contradiction
> between my private religion and the religion of
>   the rite.

This confession repeats a theme that Miłosz has accented frequently in his poetry. Let three poems suffice as examples. In one he speaks approvingly of "Helene's Religion": "On Sunday I go to church and pray with all the others. / Who am I to think I am different?" And yet, familiar disappointment in the Church rises to the surface as Helene says, "Enough that I don't listen to what the priests blabber in their sermons. / Otherwise, I would have to concede that I reject common sense."

Then, speaking for and with Miłosz himself, she continues: "I have tried to be a faithful daughter of my Roman Catholic Church. / I recite the Our Father, the Credo and Hail Mary / Against my abominable unbelief." Here the solid regularity of Catholic practice faces down Miłosz's reflexive skepticism.

In "With Her" Miłosz speaks of hearing a passage from Scripture during Mass at St. Mary Magdalen in Berkeley: "A reading this Sunday from the Book of Wisdom / About how God has not made death / And does not rejoice in the annihilation of the living." We should not be surprised that the words catch his attention. They directly address the key question that he and the gnostics often posed: how to reconcile death and innocent suffering with the notion of a good God. The poem continues: "A reading from the Gospel according to Mark / About a little girl to whom He said: 'Talitha, cumi!' " Then, with an unselfconscious humility, the poet witnesses to how he has received these words. He writes, "This is for me. To make me rise from the dead / And repeat the hope of those who lived before me." Here Miłosz is exactly a Christian—the scriptural word is received as a word for him in that moment, together with all those who have believed before him. The theological term for this is "communion of saints."

The poem "In a Parish" can serve as a third example of Miłosz's understanding of Catholic practice. He begins, "Had I not been frail and half broken inside, / I wouldn't think of them, who are like myself half broken inside. / I would not climb the cemetery hill by the church / To get rid of my self-pity." Here again is Miłosz involved in Catholic practice, the visiting of cemeteries being an especially strong part of Polish Catholicism. But he is also bringing to explicit expression what is implicit in any Christian gathering, whether among the living or the dead—namely, the recognition that we are all frail and broken. This is, among other things, what brings Christians together across differences of background. As Miłosz looks at the names on the tombs, from his own "half broken inside" he begins to establish a communion with those buried there, musing ironically on the meanings of the names he reads: "Crazy Sophies, / Michaels who lost every battle, / Self-destructive Agathas." When a child is born we name him or her with an uncomplicated hope. But then the child grows up and a sadder story must be told. Still, Miłosz sees all these lives under the sign that, for a Christian, ultimately explains existence: they all "Lie under crosses with their dates of birth and death." And in this moment the poet feels his vocation again. He asks, "And who / is going to express them? Their mumblings, weepings, hopes, tears of humiliation?" Miłosz does not answer this question in the poem, but his work as poet has always been to give voice to precisely this: all the sad, neglected stories of so many men and women.

But for Christian faith, under every cross and every sad story lies the hope of resurrection. It is this that Miłosz ultimately expresses as he gives voice to the dead. The poem ends with him addressing them all: "Thus we go down into the earth, my fellow parishioners." We may call this a sad story, but we should also note the communion expressed in going down to death with "fellows." And how do we all go down? "With the hope that the trumpet of judgment will call us by our names." Christian faith teaches that such a call will not summon us to some vague eternity. Instead, we shall be renewed as the particular persons we were meant to be, expressed mysteriously in our names, their deepest, truest meaning now revealed in the "judgment that will call us by our names." And this in the "new heavens and new earth" promised by the Scripture (2 Peter 3:13). And so Miłosz concludes,

Instead of eternity, greenness and the movement
   of clouds.
They rise then, thousands of Sophias, Michaels,
   Matthews,
Marias, Agathas, Bartholomews.
So that at last they know why
And for what reason?

These three poems may help us to understand Miłosz's ultimate message in the *Treatise*—namely, his choice to "sing with
them," his fellow Christians, despite the fact that he is naturally a skeptic, and despite his lengthy grappling with gnostic
theories.

In the last stanza of the *Treatise*, Miłosz addresses himself directly to the "Beautiful Lady, you who appeared to the children
at Lourdes and Fatima." Such a direct invocation involved a
great risk; Miłosz knew it might alienate many of his readers.
They would wonder how such a serious writer could take seriously the Marian apparitions at Lourdes and Fatima. Believing
in the authenticity of such apparitions is not even a require-
ment of Catholic faith. And yet here is Miłosz admitting, "I too
have been a pilgrim in Lourdes / by the grotto," and further,
"Lady, I asked you for a miracle." And if these revelations of
common piety upset his nonreligious admirers, he, too, was
somewhat upset by the experience: "My presence in such a
place was disturbed / By my duty as a poet who should not
flatter popular imaginings, / Yet who desires to remain faithful to your unfathomable intention / When you appeared to
children at Fatima and Lourdes."

We must take this as his last word in this long poem (that is
in fact what it is). After rehearsing all his anguished questions
and the gnostic solutions to which he had sometimes turned
along the way, he finishes with a serene prayer to the Beautiful

Lady and takes children as his model. He no longer demands a transparent solution to the problem of innocent suffering. Instead, he expresses a humbler aim: to remain faithful to the "unfathomable intention" of the mother of Christ. Miłosz had suggested earlier in this stanza that part of this intention has to do with beauty: "As if you wished to remind them that beauty is / one of the components of the world." The Lady herself is beautiful, as is the place where she appears, "in Lourdes / by the grotto, where you hear the rustle of the river and, / in the pure blue sky above the mountains, a narrow scrap of moon."

Miłosz wished to bear witness to the great Christian insight about beauty, so memorably expressed by Dostoevsky: Beauty will save the world. For Miłosz this was not an insight arrived at late in life; the *Treatise* presents us with the mature version of what we already saw in the poetry he was writing during the darkest period of the Second World War: "Gentle verses written in the midst of horror declare themselves for life." As a young poet, Miłosz knew that it was always the poet's job to record and praise the world's passing beauty. In the *Treatise*, the older Miłosz reminds us that the poet receives this beauty from a permanent source beyond the world.

If this message about beauty was indeed part of the Lady's intention, we might go on to ask whether her intention might ultimately concern the revelation of her Son as the secret of her own and the world's beauty. After all, everything about Mary leads us in this direction. Non-Catholics often worry about an excessive Catholic devotion to Mary, and in some cases the worry is justified; but in Catholic teaching and tradition— and here Miłosz is typically Catholic in making Mary his last reference—Mary, though beautiful in herself, leads us first and last to Christ, who is beautiful even in his dying. He is the Beauty that will save the world.

9   Hast Thou Considered My Servant
Faust?

David P. Goldman, August/September 2009

C RITICS often use the Bible to help explain literature,
but, on rarer occasion, literature may help us to understand the Bible. Scores of studies examine the
biblical influence on Goethe's *Faust,* which—in the prologue,
set in heaven—paraphrases the Book of Job. Job is a difficult
book for modern readers; the idea of a divine wager at the ex-
pense of a virtuous man is disturbing, and the story is all the
more opaque for its ancient setting. But just as we must know
something of Job to read *Faust,* so Goethe aids our reading of
Job. He reworks the tale in modern terms and helps us see in
Job the challenge of understanding faith and the despair we
suffer.

The modern illusion of freedom is the stuff of Goethe's
drama. Goethe was born in 1749 on the feast of St. Augustine—
an auspicious moment, for *Faust* is in some ways the great
literary realizing of Augustine's anthropology. As the leading
German Faust scholar Jochen Schmidt observes, the characterization of Faust in the work's prologue recalls Augustine's

opening declaration in the *Confessions*: "You have made us, O Lord, for yourself, and our heart is restless until it rests in you."

In order to set the problem of Job in a modern context, Goethe required a protagonist who exemplifies Augustine's restless heart, whose nourishment is not earthly and who must continue to err and strive until God leads him to clarity, as the Lord promises in the prologue. Faust is no more an Everyman— as he sometimes is characterized—than is Job, whom the Bible calls "the greatest of all the men of the East."

Paraphrasing Job, Goethe begins *Faust* in the Heavenly Court, where Mephistopheles complains that men torment each other so thoroughly that he hardly wants to bother them. In response, the Lord asks the devil if he knows "his servant" Faust, to which the devil responds, "He serves you in a curious way; not earthly are his meat and drink . . . and everything from near and far does not requite his deeply moved heart." The Lord counters, "Man will err as long as he strives." Thus begins the wager over Faust's soul.

For his poem, Goethe required a protagonist who exemplifies Augustine's restless heart because, left to their own devices, men fall into a torpor and seek unconditional rest, as the Lord tells Mephistopheles. Complacency is the characteristically modern sin. The human condition has not changed, nor can it, so long as men must die. But modern man is more susceptible to the illusion that he can mold his own identity and make his own destiny. Modern man can persuade himself that he is alone in the universe, improvising his ethics and identity as he goes along. He can fancy himself master of the universe through science. He can even imagine that brain science eventually will resolve the existential questions that have troubled his kind for millennia. Underneath this complacency lurks an antipathy to life, articulated wittily by Goethe's devil.

These conceits flourished in Goethe's world. In both so-cial and scientific terms, Goethe stood at the cusp of moder-nity. He became a literary sensation in 1774 with *The Passion of Young Werther*, the bestselling novel of the last quarter of that century. Napoleon read it in translation under the pyra-mids. Possessed of the freedom to invent his own identity, Werther sinks into morbid introspection and a hopeless love before killing himself. Faust, the mature Goethe's protagonist par excellence, very nearly does so. Faust instead fights for a life. Goethe published the first part of *Faust* in 1807, while Napoleon forced on Europe the French Revolutionary view that society could be transformed by reason, casting aside faith and tradition. The scientific revolution of the eighteenth cen-tury similarly promised to transform ordinary life—as when the French physicist Pierre-Simon LaPlace asserted that his me-chanics could ultimately make humans omniscient. Goethe's contemporaries already had absorbed the new faith in science, with fewer reservations, perhaps, than today's secularists, who have had the opportunity to encounter some of its limitations.

To place this strange new world in context, Goethe applies the marvelous conceit of inverting the premise of the Book of Job. To tempt the righteous man of Uz, the biblical Satan takes from him all that ancient man might need (wealth, children, and health). Goethe's Mephistopheles tempts Faust instead by *offering* him everything that modern man might desire. The moderns, Goethe implies, have achieved a kind of freedom unimaginable to the ancients but have become the victims of this freedom.

This parallelism between Job and Faust is deep and rich. Job was a "whole-hearted" and "upright" man who "shunned evil." Faust is free of the sin of complacency, which Goethe considers the decisive sin of the moderns. Job is lost if he overly regrets his loss and curses God; Faust is lost if he overly enjoys his boon. According to his pact with Mephistopheles, his soul is forfeit should he be so satisfied by the devil's gifts as to mourn the passing of the moment. Job mourns the loss of the children who constitute the continuity of his own life; the childless Faust struggles to embrace life—that is what he desires rather than sex, money, or fame—but he cannot find it.

Before Faust is ready for the great wager with the devil, however, he first must reject gnosticism (the idolatry of reason, the desire for occult as well as scientific knowledge); indeed, he must learn that this form of idolatry is the repudiation of life. What Oswald Spengler called *Faustian* is the spiritual affliction that Goethe's protagonist must overcome in order to be a worthy adversary for the devil. As an amateur scientist of some importance, Goethe well understood the modern world's pretensions to mastery over nature. Faust's attempt to commune through magic with the natural universe by conjuring the Earth Spirit and his shattering failure are among the work's most vivid scenes.

The beginning of Faust's salvation is his recognition that the alluring view of "utter immortal harmony" is an illusion. He asks (in Coleridge's rendering):

> Oh! how may I gaze
> Upon thee, boundless nature? where embrace thee?
> Ye fountains of all life, whose living tides
> Feed heav'n and earth: the wither'd bosom yearns
> To taste your freshness! Ye flow sparkling on,
> And yet I pant in vain.

Man sees only "the living vesture of God" (compare Psalm 102) but cannot fully comprehend nature itself, as the Earth Spirit admonishes Faust. The gnostic attempt to achieve the transcendent through penetration of the secrets of nature can only lead to despair, and it brings Faust to the point of suicide. For Faust, the search for hidden knowledge leads only to repudiation of life.

The complacency Goethe puts first on the list of offenses begins with our idolatrous worship of our own powers of discovery, our conceit that the earth is not the Lord's but ours. The new religion of science that flowered in the late eighteenth century offered the old gnosticism in a new wrapping. Unguided reason only allows man to be beastlier than any beast, as Mephistopheles quips. Complacency arises from self-worship, and that is why Goethe puts sloth at the top of the list of deadly sins.

It is thus Faust's Augustinian restlessness that allows him to be saved. He is not seduced by the false promises of the ersatz faith of gnosticism, or there would be no drama, nor does he attain faith, for at that point the drama would end. Like skaters in Stockholm harbor, who speed over the thin sea ice just fast enough to keep it from breaking, Faust stays at the frontier of faith. Crushed by his encounter with the Earth Spirit, he lifts a vial of poison to his lips but is called back to life by the sound of church bells on Easter morning. He recalls the feeling of faith although he no longer can believe himself. When his mistress Gretchen later inquires as to his religion, he offers a pantheistic deflection.

Franz Rosenzweig's characterization of Goethe sheds light on the character of Faust. Goethe's life, observed the great German-Jewish theologian, was "a passage along a ridge between two abysses. He managed to keep the solid, enduring earth firmly under his feet his whole life long. Anyone else surely would have tumbled into one of the abysses that gape on either side of the ridge, unless he was borne up by the arms of divine love that helped him to make the leap into the eternal." Like Goethe, Faust remained suspended between faith and egotism. Rosenzweig quips that Nietzsche was not so lucky. Goethe came through, "but just try to follow him."

> A little memorial plaque has been erected on this ridge, depicting Zarathustra's ascent and plunge into the depths. . . . The plaque warns any future traveler who has ascended the ridge against another attempt after Goethe's to follow Goethe's path by trusting in the stride of one's own feet, as a pure son of this earth, without the wings of faith and love.

To extend Rosenzweig's image, Faust stands between two chasms. On the one side is faith, which would make the drama irrelevant, and on the other is the worship of his own powers, which would betray him into the clutches of the devil. Faust has lost his faith in science, the idol of choice of modern man, and he says so in his first lines on stage ("I, poor fool, am as stupid as before I began to study"), concluding, "We can know nothing." Although he cannot believe, the memory, or the possibility, of belief keeps him alive. The ancient Job begins with a test of his faith; the modern Job begins by abandoning faith in the idol of science.

Faust does not have faith, but neither is he ensnared by the false surrogates for faith. He does not have life, but he desperately desires to enter into it. Faust's search for life is the subject of the tragedy proper. The failure of his search for knowledge is only a prelude to the main dramatic action, which begins with his pact with Mephistopheles. Faust feels his restlessness not as a yearning for God but as a yearning for the next best thing: life, the actual life of mankind as opposed to the poor substitute for life embodied in the search for knowledge. It has made life hateful for Faust, as he tells Mephistopheles: "Existence seems a burden to detest, / Death to be wished for, life a hateful jest."

He is ready to curse everything, in apparent emulation of Job 3:

> Cursed be the balsam of the grape!
> Cursed, highest prize of lovers' thrall!
> A curse on faith! A curse on hope!
> A curse on patience, above all!

But death still is "an unwelcome guest," observes Mephistopheles, who knows that Faust, even though he is not capable of faith, nonetheless has been saved by the memory (which is the same as the hope) of faith. He offers Faust his standard contract ("I serve you here, and you serve me in the afterlife"), which Faust rejects contemptuously:

> What can'st thou give,
> Thou miserable fiend? can man's high spirit,
> Full of immortal longings, be by such
> As thou art, comprehended?

He instead proposes an entirely different bargain:

> If ever I lay down complacent on a bed of indolence,
> Then let me be finished in that same moment.
> If by flattery you can deceive me
> Into complacent self-admiration,
> And trick me with enjoyment,
> Then let that be my last day!
> That is the bet I offer you!

What Faust now wants is not knowledge but life:

> What is apportioned to all humankind,
> Would I enjoy in my inmost self,
> Grasp the highest and lowest with my spirit,
> And bring their weal and woe into my own breast.

Mephistopheles responds to this with astonishment and contempt. Mere mortals, he tells Faust, cannot digest life:

> Believe me, who for millennia past
> Has chewed on this hard crust:
> From cradle to the grave
> No man ever has been able to digest this sourdough!
> Believe our kind: this whole
> Was made only for a God!
> He basks in light eternal.
> Us he brought down into darkness,
> While all you get is—day and night.

Mephistopheles's retort is subtle and insidious, and he offers Faust three principal temptations: first, the pure love of the innocent Gretchen; second, the classical beauty (artistic fecundity) of Helen of Troy; and third, the creation of a new land and a new people according to his desires. All these fail. Love without responsibility leads to madness, infanticide, and Gretchen's execution. The child of Faust's union with Helen is too labile to live, and his death causes Helen to fade back into darkness. And Faust's greatest temptation, reclaiming land from the sea so that a free people can "daily conquer freedom as well as life," is poisoned by the brutal means required to advance the project.

At the end, Faust's soul is carried to God by angels who sing, "We can redeem him who bestirs himself striving." Tragedy is the outcome of spiritual as well as social engineering. Neither the Romantic love of the northern tradition, nor the classical conception of beauty of the antique south, nor their union in the persons of Faust and Helen, will suffice. Worst of all is the attempt to put into practice what Goethe yearned for in his youthful poem "Prometheus"—a new man free of the sin of complacency, who "deserves freedom and life because he must conquer them every day."

This reading of Faust's character is consistent with important strands of interpretation of the Book of Job. Faust erred in attempting to wrest secrets from nature. Traditional Jewish interpretation assigns an analogous sin to Job, for the Jewish sages could not accept the idea that God would inflict such misery on an entirely guiltless man. As Rabbi Joseph Soloveitchik argued in *Halakhic Man*, Job sins by demanding a cause-and-effect explanation of his misery:

> Job, who had raged against heaven because he had sought to render an accounting of the world and erred, accepts upon himself the divine judgment. "Who is it that hideth counsel without knowledge? Therefore have I uttered that which I understood not, things too wonderful for me, which I knew not" (Job 42:3). He sinned with his proud and overly bold venture to grasp and comprehend the secret of the cosmos; he confesses and returns to God with the discovery of the mystery of the created world and of his inability to understand that mystery. "Wherefore I abhor my words, and repent, seeing I am dust and ashes."

Job has lost his wealth, children, and health, but he also has lost his confidence that he can influence God through sacrifice and other acts of propitiation. Like Faust, he has lost power over nature, and like Faust his response is to repudiate life: "Let the day perish wherein I was born, and the night in which it was said, 'There is a man child conceived.' Let that day be darkness; let not God regard it from above, neither let the light shine upon it."

Job's wife already has advised him, "Curse God and die," which Job calls "foolish." It was foolish, for ancient man perceived a remote God whose actions were indistinguishable from fate, and to curse one's fate is foolish. Job cannot accept that blind fate has harmed him, but neither can he address God, for God is a distant force to be respected but not loved.

As several critics observe, although Job's friends use the generic names for God, *Elohim* or *El Shaddai*, Job uses the personal name YHWH.

What constitutes Job's virtue under these circumstances? On the one hand, he avoids the pagan response, to curse God. On the other hand, he avoids the response of his friends, who insist that simple cause and effect must explain his predicament. Identify the sin for which God has punished you, they tell Job, and repent, and all will be well.

Soloveitchik's description of Job's sin applies to his friends better than it does to Job himself: Although Job seeks an explanation for his calamity, he refuses to accept facile explanations. He refuses to blame himself for sins he must have committed to merit such punishment, for he knows of no such sins. Neither will he curse his fate. He remains, as it were, on a ridge between two chasms, between the sinful demand to know God's innermost intent and pagan indifferentism toward God.

Job thus occupies an ambivalent position similar to Faust's. He will be satisfied neither with sinful inquiry nor with mere resignation. Job cannot resolve the tension alone, and the answer to his question comes in the form of the appearance of God himself. God does not need to provide any more answer than his presence, and it is the act of direct address of Job to God that transforms and redeems the man. That is just what God demands of Job: "Gird up now thy loins like a man; for I will demand of thee, and declare thou unto me."

Perhaps this is why both Job and Faust continue to fascinate the literary imagination. Their internal struggle, rather than the mere external circumstances of their stories, shows the travails of the best of men at the cusp of faith. If Faust were either a man of faith or a pure egoist, his character would hold no interest, and there would be no drama. If Job were a saint who suffered arbitrarily, his story would not belong in the Bible. Faust is an extraordinary man, immune to the seductions of Satan, who can be saved if he is true to the Augustinian restlessness of his heart. Faust's fight for life helps us pierce the dusty veil of ancient times and see in Job the same contention of life and death, faith and despair, that we moderns must endure.

10 | The Cursed Poets and Their Gods

Algis Valiunas, February 2012

T HE term *poète maudit*, or "cursed poet," was coined
by Paul Verlaine. His little book *Les poètes maudits*
(1884) interleaved his own honorific prose with poems by some of the poets he most esteemed but whose very
greatness assured that they were known only to the cognoscenti.
It was their obscurity—society was indifferent to them because
they were hard to understand—that prompted Verlaine to
speak of them as cursed. This cultivated sense of neglect, even
oppression, at the hands of the bourgeois philistines became
the classic pose of the avant-garde.

But the curse seemed to be as much moral and spiritual as
social, contributing to the presumption that a true artist must
suffer agonies of genius. Verlaine himself happened to be about
as cursed as they come: alcoholic, wife beater, child abuser,
jailbird, syphilitic, down-and-outer. In no small part because
of Verlaine's own harrowing life, the meaning of *maudit* has
come to include not only the troubles such poets suffer from
society but also the troubles nature inflicts on them and the
ones they inflict on themselves, body and soul.

The paradigmatic *poète maudit* was Baudelaire (1821–67).

His *Les fleurs du mal* (1857), or *The Flowers of Evil*, is the most famous book of nineteenth-century French poetry and one of the most famous in world literature. The poems, which were revolutionary in their intermixtures of the sordid and the beautiful, reflected a spiritual extremity that the modern era has long savored, one both hell-bent and heaven-storming.

Baudelaire knew his share of hell on earth, much of it self-inflicted. In his youth he took as his mistress a bald, frightful-looking, broken-down prostitute. From her he contracted the syphilis that would ravage and kill him. As he wrote to his mother at the age of thirty-three, his was a life "damned from the beginning."

Blighted loves were only part of the story. As a young dandy he tore through an inheritance that would have set him up comfortably for life, and his family appointed a legal guardian to supervise his finances, an insult that galled him to no end. Laudanum (opium dissolved in alcohol) became an addiction. He was a virtuoso at wasting time, and he loathed himself for the irremediable injury he did to his talent.

Damned from the beginning? The man who believes himself cursed tends quite naturally to blaspheme in outrage. What more does he have to lose? The section of *Les fleurs du mal* titled "Révolte" opens with a sad mockery of Christ, who was so credulous as to think his Father suffered with him in his agony. Quite the contrary, the poet declares in "Le reniement de Saint Pierre" (Saint Peter's Denial):

> —Ah! Jesus, remember the Garden of Olives!
> In your simplicity you prayed on your knees
> To the one who in his heaven laughed at the
>   sound of the nails
> That ignoble executioners drove into your living
>   flesh.

The final line of the poem trembles with Baudelaire's bitter rage: at the Father so cruel toward his trusting children, and at the children so foolish as to trust him without question. The poet finds what satisfaction he can in brazen defiance: "Saint Peter denied Jesus . . . he did well!"

The next poem in the series, "Abel et Cain," goes a step further. To turn one's back on God is insufficient; the true unbeliever must overthrow him. "Race of Cain, ascend to heaven, / And hurl God down to earth!" And "Les litanies de Satan," the third and last poem in "Révolte," serves as a hymn to the master of the cursed. Damnation on earth confers rich privilege, the poet claims. For what greater privilege can there be than to know the truth about God's injustice, which the insipid Christian believers hide from themselves?

Baudelaire did find something better in the end. Suffering cleanses, even sanctifies, he came to believe, and he turned away from Satan and toward God. "Bénédiction," which he wrote years after the Satanic verses but which is the second poem in *Les fleurs du mal*, relates the abuse the Poet (the capital is his) endures from mother, wife, and indeed everyone else he turns to in hope of finding his love reciprocated. All comes out right in the end, however, for God reserves a place of honor in heaven for the gifted and gentle soul he has chosen for this odd fate.

> "Be blessed, my God, who gives suffering
> As a divine remedy for our impurities
> And as the best and purest essence
> That prepares the strong for holy delights!"

Yet Baudelaire gave a peculiar slant to the notion of purgative suffering, one that became a reassuring consolation to countless dissipated and morally corrupted artists. Baudelaire's supreme hero, Edgar Allan Poe, whose tales he translated and whom he memorialized in two major essays, killed himself with drink, but according to Baudelaire he also enjoyed artistic triumphs lubricated by alcohol. Poe was the archetype of the *poëte maudit*, embodying a fateful combination of creative power and self-destruction.

Baudelaire had to believe in this fateful combination because his self-love demanded it. He was a hashish and opium addict who came to hate his habit but could not give it up. Yet if the visions or raptures induced by drugs enrich a poet's consciousness, then the damage they also cause would be an acceptable price to pay. The Poe he imagines intoxicated himself partly because he could not stand himself sober. Baudelaire writes in *Edgar Poe, sa vie et ses oeuvres* (*Edgar Allan Poe, His Life and Works*, 1852),

> I am told that he did not drink like an ordinary toper, but like a savage, with an altogether American energy and fear of wasting a minute, as though he were accomplishing an act of murder, as though there was *something* inside him that he had to kill, 'a worm that would not die.'

Poe's drunkenness—and by extension Baudelaire's—thus becomes a spiritual discipline of sorts.

In Baudelaire's telling, the intoxication made Poe a superior poet, which is to say, a superior man. Killing the worm gave the writing life. "I think that very often," Baudelaire wrote, "Poe's drunkenness was a mnemonic device, a deliberate method of work, drastic and fatal, no doubt, but suited to his passionate nature. Poe taught himself to drink, just as a careful man of letters makes a deliberate practice of filling his notebooks with notes." In Baudelaire's understanding, alcohol loosed imaginative forces in Poe that sobriety did not offer. "One part of what delights us today was the cause of his death," and Poe's spiritual heroism, indeed his poetic sainthood, rested in his embrace of the life-poisoning alcohol for the sake of his art.

This is how legends, and cults, get started. Baudelaire's version of Poe's life, which is in large part Baudelaire's concoction, became bohemian gospel. In the eyes of Baudelaire, Poe was downright holy: "I am adding a new saint to the martyrology; I have the story to tell of one of those glorious unfortunates, too rich in poetry and passion, who came into this lowly world, following in the footsteps of so many others, to perform the rude apprenticeship of genius among baser spirits." Venerating Poe, Baudelaire was establishing his own claim to sanctity. He is a man who rises above others to attain creative beatitude. "A tendency to mysticism," he claimed, had been part of his character since childhood.

The overwhelming tendency at this stage of his life, however, as syphilis began its final assault and he knew little time remained, was a frantic desire to change his ways—above all, to work hard every day, "blindly, without aim, like a madman," and to say his evening prayer without fail, like "a captain posting his sentinels." The final journal entry lists some "immutable rules" that he hoped would bring order and comfort: "To pray every morning to God, *the source of all power and all justice; to my father, to Mariette, and to Poe*, as intercessors; that they may give me the necessary strength to fulfill all my appointed tasks."

Time was sadly running out. Baudelaire hoped *Mon cœur mis à nu*, his final work, would be his summa; it is in fact a scattering of fragments. Paralysis struck him; he could not move; he could not speak. If life denied him, however, perhaps death did not. On his deathbed he received the last sacraments, and he died in his mother's arms, peacefully, it is said. Perhaps his life, damned from the beginning, proved blessed at the very end. If so, Baudelaire took a perilous and crooked road to get where he wanted to go.

Paul Verlaine (1844–96) adopted Baudelaire as his intercessor. "It is to Baudelaire that I owe the awakening of poetic feeling, and what is deep in me," he wrote, and his youthful discovery of Baudelaire brought sensual craving and artistic ambition surging to the surface. At the age of twenty-one Verlaine wrote, "It is Charles Baudelaire who presents the sensitive man, and he presents him as a type, or, if you like, as a *hero*." He is a seer "with his sharpened, vibrant senses, his painfully subtle mind, his intellect steeped in tobacco, his blood burned up by alcohol." Cursed indeed—but therefore blessed.

Verlaine abandoned himself to Baudelaire's heroism. Drink, to which he became addicted, made him insanely violent. He could not be trusted with absinthe in his system and sharp objects at hand. One night, when Verlaine wanted to go on drinking and his closest friend thought he'd had enough, the poet charged after his companion with a swordstick. Coming home drunk on another occasion, he demanded 200 francs from his mother and attacked her with a saber when she didn't deliver.

She got out of town, but there were other women to abuse. Threats against and attempts on the life of his wife, Mathilde, were standard poetic procedure. Verlaine couldn't be trusted with matches any more than with swords: He tried to set his wife's hair on fire. Not even his infant son was safe from his maniacal rages. Put out by a cross word from Mathilde, he picked up the three-month-old boy and hurled him against the wall.

Verlaine was twenty-seven, with a wife and a substantial poetic reputation, when the sixteen-year-old Arthur Rimbaud, the most precocious literary genius ever, wrote to him from the provinces and sent him some poems. Verlaine invited him to Paris, and the pair soon became lovers. Violence was in Rimbaud's line as well: He would carve up Verlaine's arms and legs with a knife just for sport. Supercharged, Verlaine wrote a spate of love poems. The two men combined their genius on a fragrant encomium to the anus as cynosure of beauty and sexual pleasure. Verlaine bolted from Mathilde, headed with Rimbaud to London, quarreling with him repeatedly. One quarrel prompted Rimbaud to say he was leaving Verlaine for good; Verlaine shot him in the wrist. The wound was not grave, but, probably in part because a medical examination showed evidence of recent sodomy by Verlaine, the court gave him the maximum sentence of two years of hard labor.

Prison changed Verlaine utterly; or sort of, off and on. There he wrote many of the poems in *Sagesse* (*Wisdom*, 1881), the book that proclaimed his religious conversion and made him one of the most celebrated Catholic poets of France. Like Baudelaire, Verlaine thanks God for the suffering that raised him out of the darkness. The poem "Écrit en 1875" (Written in 1875) apostrophizes the prison where his soul was put right.

> O be blessed, fortress which I left
> Ready for life, armed with sweetness and provided
> With Faith, bread and salt and a coat for the road
> So lonely, so hard and so long, no doubt,
> On which one must strive for the innocent heights.
> And may the author of grace be loved, forever!

Later in life Verlaine described the dynamic of his conversion. Christ's agony called out to Verlaine's own and made the suffering savior real and absolutely necessary for the cursed poet. "For me, Jesus is The Crucified. He is my God because he suffered, because he suffers still. I see Him before my eyes, covered with dreadful wounds, sweating in his final agony, as the peas-

ant women of Judea actually saw him." Verlaine *knows* Jesus
with the radiant intensity of a poet's vision. He *sees* him with a
cursed poet's intimate embrace of life's horror.

But Verlaine was prone to backsliding. He rushed to see
Rimbaud a month or so after his release from prison. Bar-
hopping and fierce arguments revived the beast in Verlaine. He
was not a hypocrite; he wanted to be holy, but he was too far
gone in his alcoholism and his sexual passion for Rimbaud.
Drunk, he attacked Rimbaud, and Rimbaud knocked him out
cold; peasants found the unconscious Verlaine by the riverside
the next day. In a letter to a friend, Rimbaud registered his
satisfaction in having separated Verlaine from his newfound
odious piety: "The other day Verlaine arrived in Stuttgart with
a rosary in his paws, but three hours later he had denied his
God, and made the ninety-eight wounds of our Blessed Lord
bleed again."

Verlaine struggled mightily for spiritual purchase. He read
St. Teresa and St. Thomas Aquinas and John Bunyan. He
translated English hymns. He taught at a Catholic boarding
school and was so demonstrative in his religiosity that the students nicknamed him "Jesus Christ." Literary critics called
him the most Christian poet of the nineteenth century. But he
went on drinking like a drunk. Continuing to teach became
impossible. He fell in love with one of his pupils and lived with
him after his graduation, until the young man died of typhoid
fever—another reason for Verlaine to propel himself toward
oblivion.

Verlaine yearned for a chance at normality, but he dragged
his ugly past wherever he went. When he sought reinstatement
as a Parisian civil servant—a job he had despised in younger
days—the authorities disqualified him for moral turpitude.
Poverty, degeneracy, and decrepitude were his lot from then

on. Angel and brute, he wrote, exist simultaneously in every man—Baudelaire had written in his journal of the soul pulled between God and Satan—and the religious poems would give way to the sensual, "because I must also give voice to the Beast within me."

The poet knew he was cursed, and Verlaine tried to take pleasure and pride in being among the distinguished company of heroes. In the sonnet "À Charles Baudelaire," from the 1892 collection *Liturgies intimes* (*Intimate Liturgies*), he addresses the dead poet whom he did not know but to whom he feels himself bound by ties of sanctity and sensuality.

> And if I have any right to be among your wit-
> nesses,
> It is because, in the first place, and it is because
> somewhere else,
> near the Feet joined
> First by the cold nails, then by the swooning ec-
> stasy
> Of women of sin—those so anointed,
> So kissed, mad chrism and starving kiss!
> You fell, you prayed, like me, like all
> The souls whom hunger and thirst on the way
> Pushed beautiful with hope to reach Calvary!
> Calvary just and true, Calvary where, then, these
> doubts,
> Here, there, grimaces, art, weep for their failures.
> Eh? To die simply, we, men of sin.

There are few poets of his era harder to translate, or even to construe, than Verlaine, with his gnarled syntax and elliptical sense. But he is writing here about poetic souls united in their knowledge of Christ's suffering. It is a knowledge tied to their carnal knowledge, the "cold nails" of profligate sin that have made them suffer all the more and brought them at least within reach of salvation—though the final line suggests they may have come to Calvary just to die, not necessarily to be saved. With poems such as this Verlaine claims his glorious place among the adepts of spiritual pain, and perhaps of something like hope.

This poetic glory—Verlaine was one of the great poets of the nineteenth century—came at an extortionate price. He was unhappy in just about every way possible. He recklessly bedded down with woman after woman, most of them prostitutes, and lived alternately with two, one a common whore, the other a somewhat more respectable sometime demimondaine, both of whom he loved in his fashion and wrote poems about. They all contributed to his loneliness and misery. As for diseases, venereal and otherwise, you name it, he had it: arthritis, bronchitis, gastritis, endocarditis, diabetes, cirrhosis of the liver, gonorrhea, syphilis. Four of the last nine years of his life he spent in hospitals. The damage was so extensive that the doctors could not pinpoint what killed him.

What was the real cause of his suffering? In a certain mood, Verlaine indulged in the self-pity and self-glorification of the artist rejected by the vulgar world. In a different mood, as in his sonnet to Baudelaire, he understood that his own failures caused his sufferings, and he even rejoiced in his sin because it brought him the happiness of atonement. A forced exaltation colors both these moods, though the second comes nearer the truth. There Verlaine saw that it was not simply the indifference of society that had ruined him: He had fouled his own soul.

A man's character is his fate, and Verlaine had a bad one. True enough, but in some cases that amounts to saying a man's fate is his fate is his fate. Perhaps Verlaine ought to be pitied more than reviled. Unlike Baudelaire (or Baudelaire's imagined hero, Edgar Allan Poe), for the sake of his art he did not drink or cultivate mental disorder or deliberately destroy himself. Alcohol consumed Verlaine because he was susceptible to alcoholism, and once he became addicted he was unable to stop drinking, as are many who have not a line of poetry in them. He partook of the common suffering of the children of Adam because he was a child of fallen nature and could not help himself. He needed the crucified Christ. Only such a God both endured and transcended the human agony that the malignancies in Verlaine's own nature seemed fated to impose upon him.

Of the cursed poets, Verlaine is perhaps the most sympathetic figure: Although his poetic gift marks him as extraordinary, in every other respect his weaknesses are all too human. There are heroes of exceptional stature, the greatest of whom are gods, and there are lesser heroes exemplary in their suffering precisely because of their ordinariness. Christ harrowed hell; Verlaine got stuck there. The climb up and out was too steep. Verlaine tried and tried, but he could not make it, at least not in this world.

Rimbaud (1854–91), whom Verlaine praised at length in *Les poètes maudits*, embraced the role of cursed poet as well, although without his sometime lover's admixture of redemptive hope. In his wondrous youth, the years from sixteen to twenty, when he was ablaze with poetry, he blamed Christianity for his earthly suffering. Blasphemy came as readily to him as devotion does to the millions he despised. He scrawled excremental imprecations against God on the public benches of his hometown.

Some of his poems, too, were crude acts of vandalism. Here is a stanza from "Les pauvres à l'église" (The Poor in Church):

> And all, drooling the stupid and begging faith,
> Recite the infinite complaint to Jesus

> Who dreams on high, yellowed by the livid
> stained glass window,
> Far from bad scrawny men and from wicked
> paunchy ones.

Rimbaud was not only a pagan—there are honorable and virtuous pagans—but a barbarian, a hateful despoiler of hallowed beauties.

It is of course precisely the sort of anti-Christian fury that has made Rimbaud the great hero for subsequent generations of self-styled iconoclasts. Surrealists, Beat poets, student revolutionaries, punk rockers, clever *lycéens*, and legions of the semi-educated who preen themselves on being thoroughly modern—as Rimbaud insisted we all must be—hold him in supreme reverence. His very irreverence makes him virtually divine in their eyes. He is a renegade from bourgeois proprieties, a man with the courage to give the finger to everything and everybody that stood in the way of his desires.

Rimbaud was a genius—but to what use did he put his prodigious gift? In the fragmentary "L'homme juste" (The Just Man), Rimbaud pulls out the stops as he vents his contempt for those who think themselves better than he:

> I am cursed, you know! I am drunk, crazy, livid,
> Whatever you want! But go to bed, right away,
> Just man! I want nothing from your torpid brain.
>
> . . .
>
> And you are the eye of God! the coward! When
> the cold
> Soles of divine feet would trample on my neck,
> You are a coward! O your forehead that swarms
> with lice!
> Socrates and Jesus, holy and just, disgusting!
> Respect the supreme Cursed One of bloody

nights.

There are mysteries to know, and there are gods
to worship.

To be cursed is to stand outside the circle of light where the self-righteous congratulate themselves that they are not like him. Yet it is the cursed outcast to whom the universe intimates its precious secrets. It is the cursed who is anointed.

In "Soleil et chair" (Sun and Flesh), which Rimbaud originally titled "Credo in unam," the poet swings between utter rejection of any gods whatsoever and joyous worship of pagan divinities.

—And yet, no more gods! no more gods! Man is
King,

Man is God! But Love, that is the great Faith. . . .
I believe in you! I believe in you! Divine mother,
Aphrodite from the sea!—Oh! the way is bitter
Since the other God hitched us to his cross;
Flesh, Marble, Flower, Venus, it is in you I believe!
Yes, Man is sad and ugly, sad under the vast sky,
He has clothes, because he is no longer chaste,
Because he has soiled his proud head of a god,
And he has withered, like an idol in the fire,
His Olympian body in filthy slavery.

To Rimbaud the ancient Greek gods and goddesses seem all the richer by comparison with the pallid starveling Christ. One knows the divine through the heat of sun on flesh, and the ecstasy of flesh on flesh.

In *Une saison en enfer* (*A Season in Hell*), his signature piece of visionary prose and poetry, he blames his earthly damnation on his baptism and Christian childhood and looses a proto-Nietzschean cry of hatred for the superstition that has made humanity barren, along with a cry of hope for the future that will right the wrong.

> When shall we go beyond the shores and the moun-
> tains, to salute the birth of the new work, the new
> wisdom, the flight of tyrants and demons, the end of
> superstition, to celebrate—the first!—Christmas on
> earth! The song of the heavens, the march of peoples!
> Slaves, let us not curse life.

Rimbaud believed he had found the way out of hell.

> We must be absolutely modern. No hymns. I must
> hold what has been gained. Hard night! The dried
> blood smokes on my face, and I have nothing behind
> me except that horrible tree! . . . A spiritual battle is
> as brutal as a battle of men; but the vision of justice is
> the pleasure of God alone.
>
> *. . . I shall be free to possess truth in one body and soul.*

His writing, his poetic spirit, seemed to have everything to do
with this "new wisdom." A "Christmas on earth" made it possible to endure the all-out attacks of bourgeois respectability,
the harsh whips of conventional morality, and damnation by
the Christian God. But he soon had enough of that whole
business. Evidently, after 1874, when he was twenty, he did not
write another poem. He gave up wanting the spiritual adventure of a God-abandoned, God-abandoning life, something
that he above all other modern poets is known for wanting.

Intense ambition remained, but it was directed toward the
goods that most men pursue. Rimbaud became a merchant
in East Africa, infamously running guns to a savage warlord.
He hoped to make a fortune, return to France, marry a decent
woman, father a son, and raise him to be an engineer, a solid
citizen. Matters turned out otherwise. The pile of money he
made was largely lost in the endemic African turmoil. A terrible
illness, perhaps bone cancer, ate into his leg. He made it back

to France, where amputation was performed. It did not save him. He died in Marseilles at the age of thirty-seven.

There are three basic responses to the spectacle of the cursed poets and their suffering. Artists and their rooting section have traditionally blamed the bourgeois, dubbing them philistines for their failure to understand poetry and to appreciate the emotional turbulence supposedly necessary for poetic genius to flourish. By this way of thinking, conventionality stifles true art, and therefore transgression serves as the proper path toward original rather than derivative art—and authentic rather than soulless life. Of course, this line of defense seemed more plausible in Baudelaire's day than in our own: Moral aberration is not nearly so despised now as it was then. But it endures. Indeed, the liberating fantasies of transgression now have the protections of tenure and the emoluments of endowed chairs. Rimbaud has become the poet laureate of our new bourgeois conventions.

The moralizers provide the second response. They are quite satisfied to see the literary types ruined for their wickedness. Such gratified loathing was more common in the nineteenth century than it is now, when irreligion and sexual disorderliness are not uncommon among the respectable. Nevertheless, in certain instances custom dies hard. The 1857 judicial ban on publication of six Baudelaire poems that violated public morality was not lifted until 1949, after years of efforts to get the ruling overturned. The popularity of Allen Ginsberg is often cited as proof that anything goes if you're a poet these days, but there are still many who despise him and his kind.

Neither response does justice to the cursed poets of nineteenth-century France, men whose verse did so much to shape modern literature. Truth be told, one finds it difficult to sort out the injuries that others inflicted upon them, and those they caused to themselves. Verlaine's inborn predisposition to alcoholism and the monstrous things he did while drunk; Rimbaud's abandonment by his father when he was six and his blasphemous rages against the Father who indifferently permits his children's suffering: It would take a bourgeois moralizer of the old school to condemn these men unequivocally for what they made of their lives, considering what they were given.

And yet the cursed poets were not passive victims either. Baudelaire's imagined picture of Edgar Allen Poe's drunken genius created a powerful mythology, and the cursed poets were cursed in part because they considered themselves sworn members of an elite brotherhood, an order of poets who would dare, and endure, anything for their art. Thus they came to revere as essential to their vocation the wildest transports and the most searing afflictions, whatever their origin.

One can see why the cursed poets believed they had been chosen for so terrible and sublime a fate. Their mythology of genius born in suffering helped make their hard lot endurable, as countless adolescents who have read J. D. Salinger can testify. But it also drove them deeper into misery—drove them to seek out misery, to cherish drunkenness, madness, ordeal, as a source of poetic inspiration. That wisdom comes of suffering, at least for prophets and tragic heroes, is an ancient truth; but is it wisdom to chase after suffering, as though the evil of the day were insufficient?

There is something perverse about these poets and their view of their calling. Their loneliness, drunkenness, disease, the early deaths of or abandonment by their fathers, the tauntings and beatings they took from their schoolmates: These and other blows became the fundamental truths about the world and the stuff of their poetry. They did not imitate Christ's selfless suffering. Instead, with a poet's vanity, each relished in his own way his martyrdom, championed it, flaunted it.

Baudelaire, Verlaine, Rimbaud: They were remarkable artists, yes, among the greatest of their time. But the perversity of unhappiness cherished and cultivated constricts their excellence: The pursuit of unhappiness assumed too large a place in their souls.

Yet they were better men than the twenty-first-century intellectuals who have supplanted them as cultural heroes. Baudelaire, Verlaine, and Rimbaud fought for their souls, even if theirs was not exactly a winning fight. Today's intellectuals scorn the very notion of a soul.

They loathe the religious traditions of the West, and they love to strike the pose of fearlessness before the abyss, especially after the manner of Nietzsche. Among the supposedly best-educated persons of our time, the idea of a disenchanted world, grim and cruel, has largely replaced the living spiritual reality of which poets used to sing. The *poètes maudits* have yielded to the *intellectuels maudits*. The poetry is fading, but modern men always learn new ways to curse and be cursed.

11 | George Eliot: Good Without God

ALAN JACOBS, April 2000

> *George Eliot: The Last Victorian*
> by Kathryn Hughes
> Farrar, Straus & Giroux, 400 pages, $30

O N the second day of January 1842, in a mild corner of the English Midlands, a young woman of twenty-two named Mary Ann Evans refused to attend church with her father. "Robert Evans's response," writes the young woman's most recent biographer, "was to withdraw into a cold and sullen rage." Thus began what Mary Ann called a "holy war."

The conflict had been coming for some time. Robert Evans—the agent of a large estate in Warwickshire, near Coventry—had raised his children as middle-of-the-road Anglicans, but some of his daughter's teachers, in the "ladies' seminaries" she attended from age nine, were more enthusiastic. Their evangelical piety appealed to Mary Ann, but she had not been in their world for too long before she began to perceive a dissonance between that piety and her already impressive reading in literature, theology, and science. An inner tension mounted, and culminated in a decisive recognition that she was no longer a Christian. What remained was to summon the courage to make this recognition public—which is to say, reveal it to her father. And this is what she did on the second day of January 1842.

Because of her father's silence, Mary Ann felt that she had to explain herself in a letter to him. Of the Bible she wrote,

> I regard these writings as histories consisting of mingled truth and fiction, and while I admire and cherish much of what I believe to have been the moral teaching of Jesus himself, I consider the system of doctrines built upon the facts of his life . . . to be most dishonorable to God and most pernicious in its influence on individual and social happiness.

This was scarcely calculated to assuage Robert Evans's anger, but it had the singular merit of honesty.

Nearly two years later—after father and daughter had come to imperfect but sustainable terms of peace—Mary Ann was able to write to a friend explaining what she had learned from the "holy war" and sketching the outlines of what had come to replace the traditional faith she rejected. "Speculative truth begins to appear but a shadow of individual minds," she wrote, "agreement between intellects seems unattainable, and we turn to the *truth of feeling* as the only universal bond of union." And this would remain her view. Thirty years later—after Mary Ann Evans had come to London and become Marian Evans, then (in her mind, though not in English law, since the man with whom she lived was married to another) Marian Lewes, and ultimately the great and famous novelist George Eliot—she wrote in very similar terms to Harriet Beecher Stowe: for the good of humankind, orthodox Christianity must be replaced by an ethical religion that would instill in us "a more deeply awing sense of responsibility to man, springing from sympathy with the difficulty of the human lot." Likewise, in commenting on her *Silas Marner*, she would say that it "sets . . . in a strong light the remedial influences of pure, natural, human relations."

The story, told in this way, is a remarkably familiar one: the "Victorian crisis of faith" and its resultant emphasis on the "spirit of human brotherhood" as an unarguably nonsectarian substitute for a failed religion. Why, then, must we tell it so often? Kathryn Hughes's biography is the most recent in what has become, it appears, an annual series: Rosemary Ashton's life of Eliot appeared in 1997, Rosemarie Bodenheimer's in 1996, Frederick Karl's in 1995. Do we need so many lives of Eliot? Of course not, and it is largely an accident of publishing that we now have all of these. No doubt each of them was commissioned by editors ignorant of the existence of the other projects—editors aware that no significant full biography of Eliot had appeared since Gordon Haight's authoritative volume of 1968, and that her ever-increasing stature in the pantheon of English writers certainly merited renewed biographical activity.

What is noteworthy is the relatively insignificant degree to which these biographies differ from one another. Karl's is lengthy and ponderous, Bodenheimer's critical rather than strictly biographical (and organized thematically rather than chronologically), Ashton's direct and scholarly, and Hughes's colloquial to the point of breeziness, but all of them tell more or less the same story in more or less the same terms. For (and this may be the chief lesson to be learned from these biographies) George Eliot is perhaps *the* signal figure for those who maintain that we can be good without God, indeed, that belief in the Christian God is a great impediment to the achievement of "individual and social happiness." For literary people who want to have moral standards, or at least the *feeling* of having moral standards, without accruing any metaphysical baggage, Eliot's story warrants continual regard.

One way to understand what Eliot represents is to look at her first and in some respects most beautiful novel, *Adam Bede* (1859). Near the end of the book the Methodist lay preacher Dinah Morris mistrusts her love for the carpenter Adam Bede because she cannot reconcile it with her almost lifelong sense of calling to ministry:

> Since my affections have been set above measure on you, I have had less peace and joy in God; I have felt as it were a division in my heart. And think how it is with me, Adam: that life I have led is like a land I have trodden in blessedness since my childhood; and if I long for a moment to follow the voice which calls me to another land that I know not, I cannot but fear that my soul might hereafter yearn for that early blessedness which I had forsaken; and where doubt enters, there is not perfect love. . . . We are sometimes required to lay our natural, lawful affections on the altar.

Note that Dinah does not believe her love for Adam, even if strong "above measure," to be intrinsically sinful; it is a "natural, lawful affection." And yet she feels that she may be called upon to forgo that love for the sake of a specific calling from God, for the sake, then, of a higher love—including the love of her neighbors, who might also be displaced by the avariciousness of eros: "I fear I should forget to rejoice and weep with others; nay, I fear I should forget the Divine presence, and seek no love but yours." Adam's reply to these concerns is eloquent:

> I don't believe your loving me could shut up your heart; it's only adding to what you've been before, not taking away from it; for it seems to me it's the same

> with love and happiness as with sorrow—the more we
> know of it the better we can feel what other people's
> lives are or might be, and so we shall only be more
> tender to 'em, and wishful to help 'em. The more
> knowledge a man has the better he'll do 's work; and
> feeling's a sort o' knowledge.

In other words, Dinah's love of Adam and her love of God need not compete with one another: They can be complementary forces in the expansion of Dinah's character, the strengthening of the affections that bind our lives and our neighbors' in mutual help and regard. Conversely, were Dinah to "shut up her heart" to the love of Adam, she would be sealing off one entrance for knowledge—that is to say, wisdom—and this could scarcely be pleasing to God.

One would think that Adam here speaks for Eliot herself; and in some respects, though not all, this is true. A few years earlier, before inventing George Eliot, Marian Evans had written a series of brilliant articles for London's *Westminster Review,* one of which (in October 1855) discussed a recent book by a Calvinist preacher in London, Dr. John Cumming. (Among the recent biographers Ashton best recognizes the importance of this essay, while Hughes almost ignores it.) Perhaps the angriest moment in a luminously angry essay comes when Marian Evans evaluates what she thinks of as Cumming's key claim:

> Dr. Cumming's theory . . . is that actions are good or
> evil according as they are prompted or not prompted
> by an exclusive reference to the "glory of God." God,
> then, in Dr. Cumming's conception, is a being who
> has no pleasure in the exercise of love and truthfulness
> and justice, considered as effecting the well-being of
> His creatures; He has satisfaction in us only in so far as
> we exhaust our motives and dispositions of all relation
> to our fellow-beings, and replace sympathy with men

by anxiety for the "glory of God."

Then follows a witty, indeed a gleefully malicious, catalogue of brave and noble deeds that in Dr. Cumming's scheme could give no pleasure to God. And one item in this list bears a close affinity to the dilemma of Dinah Morris, which George Eliot would delineate just three years later:

> A wife is not to devote herself to her husband out of love to him and a sense of the duties implied by a close relation—she is to be a faithful wife for the glory of God; if she feels her natural affections welling up too strongly, she is to repress them; it will not do to act from natural affection—she must think of the glory of God.

When Dinah Morris ultimately *does* agree to marry Adam Bede, then, she refuses the Cumming-like divorce between a supposedly meritorious love of God (coupled with an abstract love of one's neighbor) and a supposedly dangerous love for particular other people. That is, she rejects the picture of human affection that Marian Evans believed typical of the evangelicalism she had embraced as an adolescent and from which she felt she had been rescued by modern theology and philosophy, especially the work of David Strauss and Ludwig Feuerbach (both of whom she had translated into English). Indeed, the words with which Dinah accepts Adam's proposal explicitly join eros and agape: "My soul is so knit with yours that it is but a divided life I live without you. And this moment, now you are with me, and I feel that our hearts are filled with the same love, I have a fulness of strength to bear and do our heavenly Father's will, that I had lost before."

This is very beautiful, but the Epilogue to the novel, set seven years after the conclusion of the main narrative, reveals an interesting complication. In his wooing of Dinah, Adam had explicitly said that she need not think of marriage as an impediment to her career as a preacher, but now we find that she has after all ceased to preach. Now, this is not Adam's doing, but the doing of the Methodist Conference, which in 1803 (really, not just in the novel) forbade women from preaching. But Adam enthusiastically endorses Dinah's decision to obey the conference rather than join another denomination and continue preaching, which Adam's brother Seth believes she should have done. It is not clear that devotion to God and devotion to Adam have proved utterly compatible after all. It may well be that Dinah's former quest for divine love has simply been absorbed into the concerns and affections of everyday life; that, faced with the joyful obligation to love Adam and their children, she has found less need to project a God as the ideal and source of love.

The word "project" inevitably and rightly calls to mind Feuerbach's "projection theory" of religion. Marian Evans's critique of Dr. Cumming is conducted on purely Feuerbachian principles, and the closing paragraphs of her essay are almost a précis of *The Essence of Christianity*:

> The idea of God is really moral in its influence—it really cherishes all that is best and loveliest in man—only when God is contemplated as sympathizing with the pure elements of human feeling, as possessing infinitely all those attributes which we recognize to be moral in humanity. . . . The idea of a God who not only sympathizes with all we feel and endure for our fellow men, but who will pour new life into our too languid love, and give firmness to our vacillating purpose, is an extension and multiplication of the effects produced by human sympathy.

To this useful image Marian Evans contrasts Dr. Cumming's

God, who

> instead of sharing and aiding our human sympathies
> is directly in collision with them; who instead of
> strengthening the bond between man and man, by
> encouraging the sense that they are both alike the
> objects of His love and care, thrusts himself between
> them and forbids them to feel for each other except as
> they have relation to Him.

Perhaps, then, the Epilogue to *Adam Bede* is to be read as documenting Dinah's escape from the clutches of this ugly and dangerous notion of God. If Dinah gives up preaching in order better to love her husband, children, and friends, she has simply demonstrated the moral self–sufficiency and maturity that Feuerbach and Marian Evans envision as the future of the human race. We can now see how this view differs quite distinctly from that of Adam Bede himself: for Adam, the love of God and the love of others are mutually reinforcing, while for Marian Evans the love of God, or rather the whole notion of God, has a strictly instrumental function and can safely be abandoned when it is no longer needed as a stimulus to the love of one's fellow humans.

I believe Adam's position on this issue to be superior to that of the mature Marian Evans—though earlier in her life, when she was still Mary Ann Evans, she had still thought orthodox Christian doctrine to be "dishonorable to God" as well as injurious to people. But in any case, one consequence of the view Marian Evans came to articulate is that, for all the broad human sympathy for which she became justly famous, in one respect her sphere of sympathetic engagement contracted—namely, in the realm of religious experience.

The pious evangelicals whom she had represented so faithfully and with such warmth in her early work disappear from her later fiction. In *Felix Holt* (1866) the evangelical world makes something of a return, but with notably less success. In *Middlemarch* (1872), its only representative is the wretched Mr. Bulstrode with his secret past of vice—a touch too predictable for the creator of Dinah Morris. Even in Eliot's last novel, *Daniel Deronda*, with its remarkable and unprecedented portrayal of Jews in England, it is the ethics of Judaism that she—like Matthew Arnold with his notion of the Hebraic "strictness of conscience"—admires, not its metaphysics. In a letter she tells a friend that Christians owe Jews respect because of their "professed principles," principles she hoped would someday be embodied in a Palestinian Jewish state. A Zionism born of *haskalah* (the Jewish enlightenment) comprises Eliot's portrait of excellent Judaism; the beliefs and worship of Jews are but exotic window dressing.

This waning of sympathy for religious experience is vividly evident in her comments on Newman's *Apologia Pro Vita Sua*: the book was "the revelation of a life—how different in form from one's own, yet with how close a fellowship in its needs and burthens." One would think the book was the autobiography of a Melanesian, so loftily distant is her response; it is the response of a person who knows certain moral stirrings (stemming from "needs and burthens") but who knows better than to project a God from them. I am tempted, when confronted by this attitude, to invoke Nietzsche's scathing comment, in *Twilight of the Idols*, on the difference between the English and the Germans:

> G. *Eliot.*—They have got rid of the Christian God, and now feel obliged to cling all the more firmly to Christian morality: that is *English* consistency, let us not blame it on little bluestockings la Eliot. In England, in response to every little emancipation from theology

> one has to reassert one's position in a fear-inspiring manner as a moral fanatic. That is the *penance* one pays there. With us it is different. When one gives up Christian belief one thereby deprives oneself of the *right* to Christian morality.

This is, like most of what Nietzsche wrote, unfair: Eliot was neither a "little bluestocking" nor a "moral fanatic," and moreover drew almost all of her ideas about how to sustain Christian morality without Christian belief from reading Germans like Strauss and Feuerbach. More important, Nietzsche underrates the courage required to make even the effort to sustain moral commitment on such terms. It is Eliot's unwavering earnestness in that effort that leads Hughes to call her "the last Victorian," that is, the last person to believe wholly in the Victorian project of public and private virtue. Faced with the widening cracks in the social and personal foundations of her world, "George Eliot was the last Victorian who believed that it was possible to face these kinds of crises without shattering into shards."

But while Nietzsche's comment is unfair it is also deeply perceptive: Eliot does become ever more passionate about the moral life as her belief in anything transcendent evaporates. Yet events since Eliot's death have revealed with excessive clarity the impossibility of sustaining Christian morality without Christian belief. Nietzsche was indeed prophetic on this score: Early in his career he wrote an essay on Strauss that remains to this day an unmatched evisceration of liberal Protestantism, its easy conscience and unfounded cheerfulness.

Perhaps, though, we should not end by noting that Eliot had less foresight than Nietzsche. Would that her hopes had been better justified! And there will always remain something lovely about the earnestness with which her characters pursue their vision of goodness. One thinks of the beautiful but frivolous

Gwendolen Harleth at the moment she realizes that Daniel Deronda will marry someone else:

> The world seemed getting larger round poor Gwendolen, and she more solitary and helpless in the midst. . . . That was the sort of crisis which was at this moment beginning in Gwendolen's small life: she was for the first time feeling the pressure of a vast mysterious movement, for the first time being dislodged from her supremacy in her own world. . . . Here had come a shock that went deeper than personal jealousy—something spiritual and vaguely tremendous that thrust her away, and yet quelled all anger into self-humiliation.

For all in our spiritual lives that Eliot came to be blind to, she has few equals as a discerner—and a celebrator—of the small and large mutations of our moral lives. This is much to be grateful for, though the cause of that gratitude can be seen more clearly in Eliot's novels than in the stories her biographers (competent though they be) have woven. As long as even a handful of scholars continue to find her pursuit of goodness attractive, there is hope even for the nearly blighted groves of academe.

12 | The Moral Witness of Aleksandr Solzhenitsyn

DANIEL J. MAHONEY, October 2009

W HEN his passing a few years ago—on August 3, 2008, at the age of eighty-nine—the world was obliged to come to terms once again with Aleksandr Isaevich Solzhenitsyn. It was time to sum up and take stock of the Russian Nobel laureate, antitotalitarian writer, and courageous if unnerving moral witness. The response was more abundant and on the whole more respectful than one might have anticipated.

Still, there was something disturbingly anachronistic about the American and British commentary. Although most commentators understood that Solzhenitsyn had played a truly decisive role in bringing down an "evil empire" and paid tribute to *The Gulag Archipelago* as a book that told essential truths about communism, almost all highlighted his 1978 Harvard address and his status as a *dissident* (a word he never used to describe himself), and they were inordinately concerned with his judgments about the Yeltsin and Putin years. In writing about his recent political views, they relied more on recycled news accounts than on an examination of his own speeches and writings.

And there were more egregious offenders. A lengthy obituary in the *New York Times* was laden with factual errors and repeated every possible cliché about Solzhenitsyn's political and religious convictions, and said nothing of substance about his major literary projects over the past twenty years. An otherwise respectful article in *The Economist* suggested that his fierce criticism of the criminal oligarchy of the Russian 1990s was rooted in personal pique: Solzhenitsyn, against all evidence, was said to have yearned for political power for himself. Professional Solzhenitsyn bashers Cathy Young (in the *Boston Globe*) and Zinovy Zinik (in the *Times Literary Supplement*) argued that Solzhenitsyn's legacy was "tarnished," that he had become the theoretician of Putin-style authoritarianism and even a quasi-fascist.

The Western commentary that followed Solzhenitsyn's death captured little of the complexity or nuance of Solzhenitsyn's political judgment after his return to Russia in May 1994. Tendentious commentators never discussed his detailed proposals for building democratic self-government in Russia from the bottom up, proposals that are at the heart of his political vision, as articulated in *Rebuilding Russia* (1990), *Russia in Collapse* (1998), and the luminous speeches and addresses collected in *A Minute Per Day* (1999).

Most commentators missed that Solzhenitsyn's support for a broad "social restoration" in Russia after 2001 was not uncritical support for the Putin regime. He openly criticized the party-dominated character of the Russian legislature, the lamentably slow development of local self-government in his homeland, the massive corruption in private and public life. He argued that the government ought to do much more to encourage entrepreneurial capitalism by supporting vigorous independent small- and medium-size businesses.

He worried about the failure of democracy—particularly the "democracy of small spaces"—to take root in his beloved Russia. He was convinced that local self-government of the Swiss or New England variety would be a "welcome solution" and an outlet for the energy of ordinary, decent citizens. As the article he was working on at the time of his death attests (see "Fugitives from the Family," *Rossiyskaya Gazeta*, December 11, 2008), he was particularly concerned about the estrangement of contemporary Russians from the millennium-old spiritual patrimony of the nation, a patrimony that had bequeathed to them faith in God, "a free, rich, and vivid language," and "traditions of home and business life."

He was not a nationalist in the narrow sense of the term, but he was deeply committed to the preservation of Russian "national consciousness." While he welcomed the restoration of Russian national pride, or self-respect, during the Putin years—and categorically repudiated imperialism or foreign adventurism—he parted from the Russian government's increasing refusal to confront the monstrous character of the Soviet past.

Yet even sympathetic commentators tended to miss the high-mindedness of Solzhenitsyn's concerns, which presupposed a breadth and depth of perspective that one can only characterize as philosophic. For the most part, the writings that have appeared over the past two or two and a half decades remain unknown in the United States, and his chef d'oeuvre, *The Red Wheel*, is far more talked about than read. The crucial volumes dedicated to the revolutionary upheavals of February and March 1917 are still unavailable in English. So it is necessary to turn abroad for deeper treatments and appreciations. In an important new book, *Le Phénomène Soljénitsyne*, published at the beginning of 2009, the French Russianist Georges Nivat incisively analyzes Solzhenitsyn's achievement as an innovative writer and penetrating moral thinker who recovered old but enduring verities in the age of ideology.

Nivat argues that two peaks—two immense "cathedrals"—dominate the Solzhenitsynian literary universe: *The Gulag Archipelago* and *The Red Wheel*. The first is a unique "experiment in literary investigation" that tells the truth about Soviet repression after 1917 even as it profoundly follows the soul's confrontation with "barbed wire." The second (coming in at 6,000 pages) combines literary innovation with dramatized history worthy of Thucydides. These two works differ in tone and style but nonetheless form a diptych.

There was nothing fated or inevitable about the Russian revolutions of 1917. But through certain choices or the lack thereof, the "red wheel" began to turn with something like cosmic intensity. Its destination was "the gulag archipelago," the massive system of Soviet repression centered around the forced labor-camp system. In this diptych, Solzhenitsyn establishes beyond a reasonable doubt that the gulag flowed logically and in that sense inexorably from Lenin's self-proclaimed project to "purge Russia of all the harmful insects," to eliminate the real or imagined enemies of a quasi-mythological socialism.

Nivat also suggests, rightly, that *The First Circle* forms a third peak, or cathedral, of Solzhenitsyn's achievement. It is a great "European novel" that speaks to both the West and the East and to the broader meaning and sources of the Soviet tragedy, while never losing sight of the ultimate human questions.

The publication by HarperCollins this October of *In the First Circle* (the book's original title) in a restored ninety-six-chapter version, is therefore a publishing event of the first order. Available for the first time in English, the work is splendidly translated by Harry T. Willets and includes a thoughtful and informative foreword by Edward E. Ericson Jr. Solzhenitsyn composed *In the First Circle* between 1955 and 1958, after spending many years in prison, labor camps, and internal exile, but it underwent an extensive process of "softening" and "hardening" before a "distorted," or self-censored, version was published in the West in 1968.

The restored version is in some important respects a new work. Nine chapters are completely new and twelve substantially altered. Moreover, more than the earlier translations, Harry T. Willetts's rendering of the work captures the rhythm and idiom of the original. As a result, we are now in a much better position to judge Solzhenitsyn's achievement.

Its setting is a privileged scientific-research prison, a *sharashka*, on the edge of the gulag system—the Marfino sharashka in the Moscow suburbs where Solzhenitsyn spent three years as a prisoner between 1947 and 1950. This is the real and metaphorical "first circle" of hell to which its Dante-inspired title refers. But the work is misread if it is reduced to "gulag fiction," as if Solzhenitsyn's only purpose was to expose the infernal operations of the Soviet system of political repression.

This self-described "polyphonic" novel is above all dialogical: As in a Platonic dialogue or a Dostoevskian novel, there is no absolutely controlling or simply authoritative authorial voice. It is characterized by a complex narrative structure that combines the third-person point of view with the subjectivity that belongs to a first-person narrative. Different characters take turns as the focus of a chapter or series of chapters in the book. Solzhenitsyn's novelistic polyphony respects the variety of perspectives and voices while inviting readers to join in the search for truth. At the same time, one of the main characters, the young Gleb Nerzhin, thirty-one years of age and five years "in the harness" as the action unfolds, is a faithful literary representation of the young Solzhenitsyn and the spokesman for his own deepest convictions at the time.

The principal characters include Nerzhin and the talented Soviet diplomat Innokenty Volodin, as well as Nerzhin's closest friends and principal interlocutors, Lev Rubin and Dmitri Sologdin, who are based on the real-life figures Lev Kopelev and Dmitri Panin. Rubin, a linguist and steadfast communist, is torn between his humane instincts and his uncompromising commitment to revolutionary principles. Sologdin, an engineer, is a fierce opponent of the communist regime and a self-described Christian individualist (his Christian convictions are much more pronounced in the new version). A host of other characters, from the half-blind janitor Spiridon (whose moral good sense owes nothing to philosophical reflection) to Stalin, provides a brilliant picture of Soviet society from top to bottom.

Perhaps the most significant change is that the new chapters clarify the intellectual metanoia of the diplomat Volodin, whose dramatic phone call sets the entire plot in motion. In the first version, he calls a doctor friend to warn him that the authorities would see sharing a lifesaving medical discovery with doctors from the West as an act of treason.

In the new version, Volodin calls the American embassy to warn about an act of nuclear espionage about to occur in New York (this part of the plot is based on the case of the Soviet spy Georgy Koval). It is Christmastime in the West, the year is 1949, and the naval attaché who takes the call at the understaffed embassy speaks poor Russian and is suspicious of the information. The young diplomat's heroic act is seemingly for naught. In both versions, his call is recorded by the secret police, and the scientist prisoners in the Marfino sharashka are given the task of using the new science of *phonoscopy*, or voice identification, to track down the caller.

As Georges Nivat shows in an authoritative 1980 essay on Solzhenitsyn's "Different Circles," the new opening decisively transforms the meaning and import of Volodin's act. He is moved by "active hatred of the communist regime." He self-consciously "betrays" the regime he represents. Solzhenitsyn thus raises the question of whether one is obliged to honor the commands of a truly perverse regime. Nivat is not wrong to compare this problematic to "the medieval disputations on the legitimacy of tyrannicide" or, one might add, to Aristotle's famous question in *The Politics* about whether the good man is the same as the good citizen.

The new version thus begins by raising a question of political philosophy that became all the more pressing under conditions of totalitarianism. (It should be added that the patriot Solzhenitsyn always refused to identify the Leninist-Stalinist regime with the cause of Russia or to succumb to the charms of "Great Soviet patriotism.")

Among the principal characters in the novel, Volodin and Nerzhin stand out because their fidelity to conscience ultimately leads them to imprisonment in the gulag labor camps. Nerzhin refuses to participate in a project that will buy him time in the sharashka because it will ensnare innocent people and will detract him from the "passion" that has come to grip him, passion for the contemplation of the truth and the cultivation of his soul.

Nerzhin is recognizably the same character in the two versions of *In the First Circle*. Volodin is an even more interesting and weighty character in the new version. In both versions, he moves from being a privileged, carefree, and cosmopolitan member of the Soviet elite to being troubled by a growing aversion to the regime he had hitherto served without qualms. A crucial flashback in "But We Are Given Only One Conscience, Too," one of the most important chapters, reveals the inner transformation that led to his estrangement from his wife, the daughter of the public prosecutor in Moscow, and his decision to make the life-altering phone call.

Too nervous to attend a party at the home of his in-laws a mere twenty-four hours after the call, he reflects on the first six years of his marriage where "no inhibitions, no obstacles" were allowed to "come between wish and fulfillment." Eager "to sample every new, exotic fruit," he and his wife have as their motto an Epicurean one (at least in the vulgar sense): "We are given only one life!"

In his sixth year of marriage, he had reached a dead end. The life of endless novelty and material pleasure began to "disgust" him. His soul was ripe for self-examination. One day he "had the amusing idea of reading what his 'master' had in fact taught." Searching through his late mother's cabinets he found not only a book of Epicurus's sayings but also her letters and diaries.

He had always admired, even idolized, his father, a revolutionary naval officer who had been killed in 1921 repressing an independent peasant rebellion in Tambov province. He discovered that his "bourgeois" mother had thought deeply and widely about matters—"Truth, Beauty, Goodness, the Ethical Imperative"—that had no place in the "progressive" Soviet world that had shaped his soul. "Something he had lacked"—a moral anchor, a principled point of view—was "stealing into his heart."

His discovery of the moral law (in his mother's words, "Injustice is stronger than you . . . but let it not be done through you") led him to rethink the claims made for the Bolshevik revolution. His work as a "diplomat"—the secret meetings, the code names, the passing on of instructions and money—began to seem sordid, distasteful, repellant.

In some of the most important words of the book, Solzhenitsyn writes: "The great truth for Innokenty used to be that we are only given one life. Now, with the new feeling that had ripened in him, he became aware of another law: that we are given only one conscience, too. A life laid down cannot be reclaimed, nor can a ruined conscience."

Here, with the full force of his art, Solzhenitsyn chronicles the "existential" recovery of those elemental moral experiences that give evidence of the moral law and that give the lie to every ideological denial of the soul's connection to goodness and truth and its responsibility before them.

In the next chapter, "The Uncle at Tver," which immediately follows Volodin's repudiation of epicureanism, the restored version gives more insight into Volodin's remarkable spiritual and political transformation. Eager to know more about his mother and to connect to her past, Volodin visits her sole remaining relative, Uncle Avenir.

A handyman supported by his wife, who works as a hospital nurse, Avenir is a free man who maintains his moral integrity by, as much as possible, opting out of a system that wars against the human conscience. His home, little more than a patched-together hovel, is filled with camouflaged old newspapers that tell the truth about the Bolshevik revolution of 1917 and thus expose the lies about the past to which the Soviet people are daily subjected.

Avenir repeats the question of the nineteenth-century Russian thinker Herzen about the limits of patriotism, of loyalty to a regime intent on "destroying its own people." He sees the Second World War as a tragedy in which the Soviet people struggled heroically for the homeland only to be ground down

by "the man with the big moustache." He is convinced that
the Soviet regime could never obtain the atomic bomb by itself
but that it will resort to espionage and thievery to do so, and
that the people of the Soviet Union would then lose all hope
for freedom.

The meeting with Avenir stiffens Volodin's resolve and cures
him of any remaining ideological illusions. He is determined
to make up for the sins of the father by doing what he can to
prevent an odious regime from attaining the atomic bomb. The
Epicureans of old eschewed politics and attempted to cultivate
their private "gardens," but he now sees that to do so in the
context of an ideological regime that relentlessly wars on the
bodies and souls of human beings is to become complicit in
evil, to risk permanent spiritual corruption.

Volodin thus follows the dictates of conscience and takes a
stand for his country and humanity and against the totalitarian
regime he is officially committed to uphold. But after doing
so he is desperately afraid of being exposed and is even more
worried that his call was for naught. He knows he was right
to try to prevent "the Transformer of the World, the Forger of
Happiness, from stealing the bomb," but he is not sure that the
West deserves to be saved or is capable of acting on the warning.
And will ordinary Soviets, herded together and subject to the
most mendacious propaganda, appreciate what was at stake in
his "treasonous" act?

Several chapters near the end of the work chronicle
Volodin's arrest, interrogation, and imprisonment. These
chapters mirror Solzhenitsyn's own experience after his arrest
in February 1945. If Nerzhin is Solzhenitsyn's authorial
alter ego, Volodin's intellectual and spiritual transformation
parallels his intellectual and spiritual "ascent" as described
in *The Gulag Archipelago* and elsewhere in his work. The

newly modified conclusion of one of the last chapters, "Second Wind," takes on added importance in this regard.

Volodin now recognizes that "he would have done no other. He could not have remained indifferent." Uncle Avenir's spirited wisdom is contrasted with Epicurus's "stupid" thought that "our feelings of satisfaction and dissatisfaction are the highest criteria of good and evil." The ancient philosopher's refined, apolitical hedonism, his carefully calibrated weighing of pleasures and pain, can provide no principled ground for refusing the tyrant's claim that his pleasure is good. "Stalin, for instance, enjoyed killing people—so that, for him, was 'good'?" Those "who are imprisoned for the truth get no satisfaction from it—so is that evil?"

Epicureanism represents a dead end, a spiritual obtuseness of the first order to the imprisoned Volodin. "The great materialist's wisdom" now "seemed like the prattle of a child." "Good and evil were now distinct entities, visibly separated by that light gray door, those olive green walls, and that first night in prison." This was the decisive metanoia, the discovery of a moral universe, of the real divide between good and evil. Volodin eloquently articulates the heart of Solzhenitsyn's mature moral vision.

Nerzhin exemplifies another aspect of that moral vision, the skeptical resistance to ideologies in service of a search for truth. The dissident communist Lev Rubin, who has been unjustly imprisoned but still wholeheartedly identifies with the cause of revolutionary socialism, urges him to "look at things in historical perspective," by which he means the "inevitability" that allegedly conforms "to the inherent laws of history."

For his part, Nerzhin is a self-described skeptic whose skepticism is directed first and foremost at ideological fanaticism. This is even more apparent in the restored version of *In the*

First Circle. He wonders how he could have once "worshiped" Lenin, whose dogmatism and fanaticism are unworthy of a decent and reflective human being. But skepticism is not enough, intellectually or morally. It is useful as a way of "silencing fanaticism" but it cannot give a man a reliable footing to stand on.

But as the important restored chapter "Top-Secret Conversation" makes clear, Nerzhin had already moved significantly beyond skepticism to a much more substantial affirmation of justice, conscience, and self-limitation. Rubin warns him about the foolhardiness of "getting in the way" of the movement of history and derides him as "*Pithecanthropus erectus,*" an ape-man out of touch with the requirements of history.

Nerzhin refuses to accept this terminology or to become imprisoned by ideological abstractions. He will have nothing to do with "blasted fanatics" who refuse to give human beings space to live and breathe. He roots his opposition to fanaticism in "moral self-limitation" and mocks the Marxist idea that justice is nothing but a "class-conditioned idea." In a beautiful cri de coeur he proclaims that "justice is the cornerstone, the foundation of the universe! . . . We are born with a sense of justice in our souls; we can't and don't want to live without it!"

In the late chapter "On the Back Stairway," Nerzhin, who is about to be shipped off to the gulag, has a clandestine conversation with Illarion Gerasimovich, an engineer serving his second term of incarceration. Gerasimovich has unbounded confidence in the power of a technical or scientific elite to govern the world. He places his hope in a revolution that will bring the true men of science to power.

Nerzhin has no time for "the rational society"—the enemy of all reason and decency—and knows that there is no technical political solution that can bypass the need for human beings to live well with their freedom. He emphatically repudiates the modern ideology of progress, since it conflates moral and technical progress and turns a blind eye to the human capacity for evil, a capacity made worse by "beautiful" modern ideas. There is no "backward and forward in human history," Nerzhin tells Gerasimovich. Rather, history is "like an octopus, with neither back nor front."

Nerzhin remains committed to a life of reflection about human nature and the order of things, wedded to a conception of human dignity that does justice to the moral nature of man. He is now able to affirm certain truths that further open his eyes. The philosophical affirmation of natural justice, the experience of the soul that the good is not unsupported, is a precondition of Solzhenitsyn's recovery of faith which is described with great luminosity in the central section of *The Gulag Archipelago*: "The Soul and Barbed Wire." Solzhenitsyn's mature thought is best described as a philosophical Christianity that never loses sight of the philosophical metanoia, as described in both Volodin and Nerzhin's transformations in the full version of *In the First Circle*.

In the restored version of Solzhenitsyn's novel, readers confront a subtle thinker and gifted writer who sees in philosophical friendship and dialogue, in the rich interplay of voices and worldviews, an essential element of the soul's ascent to truth. *In the First Circle* solidly establishes the continuity of Solzhenitsyn's thought with the deepest and most humane currents of classical and Christian thought.

For fifty years or more, Aleksandr Solzhenitsyn's life and art bore witness to his confident belief, so eloquently expressed in his Nobel Prize lecture, that art could "defeat the Lie," that "one word of truth" could finally "outweigh the whole world." With the publication of the restored version of *In the First Circle*, we have an opportunity to rise to Solzhenitsyn's challenge and again to take him seriously as an artist and thinker of the first rank.

81193728R00117

Made in the USA
Columbia, SC
26 November 2017